Perseverance

The Woman on the Cover

The striking photograph of Mrs. Marie Lynthecom on the front cover is from the Thomas Cronise collection of Salem residents, taken in the mid 1900s. The picture of her with her husband and son on page 231 is from the Oregon Historical Society's collection of photos.

We know little about Marie, except through what we have learned about her husband, primarily from census records. A 1900 census shows Marie and Owen L. Lynthecom living in Kentucky. Army records indicate that Owen was from Chicago and served in the Spanish-American War as a corporal in Company D of the Eighth Infantry.

Owen Lynthecom and Marie Ellis were married on April 20, 1895, in Cook County, Illinois. According to the 1910 census, the couple had moved to Portland along with their eight-year-old son, Owen Jr.

A December 20, 1913, article in The Advocate *indicates that Owen "was employed in Salem in the office of Governor Oswald West, had two residences in Portland, one in Salem and a farm in Marion County."*

A convention bulletin lists Owen as one of the delegates from Oregon at an "Exhibition and Celebration to Commemorate the 50th Anniversary of the Emancipation of the Negro" held in Chicago August 22, 1915.

By 1920, the Lynthecom family was living in San Diego, California. No other children are recorded.

Perseverance

A History of
African Americans
in Oregon's
Marion and Polk
Counties

Oregon Northwest Black Pioneers

Salem, Oregon

—

Cover photo: Marie (Mrs. Owen) Lynthecom, 1917. Courtesy of Oregon Historical Society (OrHi bb06951)

Written and designed by Sheridan McCarthy and Stanton Nelson of Meadowlark Publishing Services. Research by Oregon Northwest Black Pioneers. Please direct requests for readings and presentations to ONWBP.

The information presented here comes from the best sources available to Oregon Northwest Black Pioneers at press time. If you have authoritative information that differs, we would be very interested in hearing from you. We will post any resulting corrections on our website and may also include them in subsequent printings.

Printed in the United States of America.
ISBN 978-1-4507-4878-0
Published 2011

Published by Oregon Northwest Black Pioneers
117 Commercial Street NE, Suite 210
Salem, OR 97301
www.oregonnorthwestblackpioneers.org

Perseverance

A History of
African Americans
in Oregon's
Marion and Polk
Counties

Oregon Northwest Black Pioneers

Salem, Oregon

—

Cover photo: Marie (Mrs. Owen) Lynthecom, 1917. Courtesy of Oregon Historical Society (OrHi bb06951)

Written and designed by Sheridan McCarthy and Stanton Nelson of Meadowlark Publishing Services. Research by Oregon Northwest Black Pioneers. Please direct requests for readings and presentations to ONWBP.

The information presented here comes from the best sources available to Oregon Northwest Black Pioneers at press time. If you have authoritative information that differs, we would be very interested in hearing from you. We will post any resulting corrections on our website and may also include them in subsequent printings.

Printed in the United States of America.
ISBN 978-1-4507-4878-0
Published 2011

Published by Oregon Northwest Black Pioneers
117 Commercial Street NE, Suite 210
Salem, OR 97301
www.oregonnorthwestblackpioneers.org

To all the African Americans—those remembered and those lost to history—who helped shape the communities of Oregon's Marion and Polk counties.

Contents

Thanks

For their generous support:
Salem Electric
Spirit Mountain Community Fund
Marion Cultural Development Corporation
Tom and Virginia Green
Black United Fund of Oregon
Oregon Northwest Black Pioneers
Pioneer Trust Bank

Gratitude to:
Salem Multicultural Institute
Kylie Pine and Amy Vandergrift of the
Willamette Heritage Center
(Marion County Historical Society)
Polk County Historical Society
Benton County Historical Society
Oregon Historical Society
Friends of the Salem Pioneer Cemetery
Hayesville Cemetery
The Statesman Journal
Oregon State Library
Willamette University
Oregon State University
Salem Public Library
Elizabeth McLagan for her encouragement and inspiration
Dr. Darrell Millner for academic consulting and advice
Mary Beth Corrigan for extensive research on
wagon train arrivals
Erika Huckestein, Ross Sutherland, Virginia Green, and
Donna Atto for research

Thanks

Mary Elizabeth Harper for research support
Kim Moreland for photographic research
Erin Zysett for her support
William Tebeau and family for interview and photos
Claudia Thompson for research,
personal stories, and photos
Dinah, Jan, and Pam Kinney for their support and their
kind donation of the Obed Dickinson coverlet
Dave Vanderhoff, Malinda Johnson, and the Salvation Army
of Salem for information on Annie Smith
Pastor Gussie Brown and Bishop Arthur Shankle for
their personal accounts of churchgoing in Salem
David and Coralee Rhoten for their kind donation of Marian
Anderson concert materials and David's personal stories
The Stephen Zielinski Family for working with us
to uncover the John W. Jackson story
Gaius and Martha Fuson and Louise Fuson Shepard
for migrant camp artifacts
John Ritter for information on the KKK
Brian Waldo Johnson for information on America Waldo
Geraldine Hammond for her personal stories
Carole Smith for photographs of the Opera House
Terri Tower and Laurie Bridges for
their research on Carrie Halsell Ward
Judy Juntunen, Patricia Benner, and Mary Gallagher for
information on Hannah and Eliza Gorman
Elizabeth Potter for her help with the
Salem Pioneer Cemetery map
Willie Richardson and Gwen Carr for
their perseverance in support of this project

Special thanks go to Sheridan McCarthy and
Stanton Nelson of Meadowlark Publishing Services
for their writing, editing, and guidance throughout
the creation of this book.

Preface

The Oregon Northwest Black Pioneers' first publication, a twenty-four-page booklet of the same name, concluded with a promise:

> ... This booklet is only one step in a larger project. It is our intention to expand, amend, and refine this project until it portrays a more complete and more accurate account of the true extent of the contributions of African Americans.

The slim volume contained a mix of information: portraits of some of Oregon's early black settlers; thumbnail sketches of life in Portland from 1870 through the 1940s; an account of the emergence of the shipbuilding town of Vanport—and the flood that destroyed it; and brief descriptions of the state's African American newspapers, among other items of interest. It was a good first step.

Sometime after publication, as happens with many all-volunteer groups, the organization lay dormant for a time. When a fresh set of volunteers brought it back to life several years later, we renewed our commitment to gathering information on African Americans throughout the state and presenting our findings to the public. We researched, organized exhibits and displays, and made presentations at schools, libraries, and other venues. And we vowed to return to publishing as part of our outreach efforts, this time with a full-length book.

Much had already been written about the black history of
Multnomah County, and we wanted to bring to light information that was not so well known. We turned our attention to
the other twenty-nine (of thirty-six) Oregon counties where
we had uncovered an African American presence—a population of one in some cases, but a presence nonetheless. Captur-
ing in a book everything we had found across such a wide
geographical area, however, was a daunting prospect.

Ultimately, Salem's Friends of Pioneer Cemetery provided our jumping-off point. They had already meticulously
documented all available information about Marion County's
black citizens who were buried at the cemetery, whether in the
form of a single line of obituary or a biographical account of
some kind. Given such a solid base, a book on Marion County seemed doable. But we couldn't quite confine ourselves
to Marion. We had discovered stories about black citizens
who lived across the Willamette River in neighboring Polk
County that were just too good to pass up. And so we settled
on creating a chronicle of the African American history of
both counties.

The adventure we embarked upon would take several
years to complete. To be frank, had we known ahead of time
the scope of work involved in pulling a book together, we
might not have been quite so excited about getting started. But
now that *Perseverance* is a reality, it is easy to see the value of
the effort that went into its making. The history of the African
American people of Marion and Polk counties—so far as it is
known today—is no longer the sole possession of the Oregon
Northwest Black Pioneers. Its distribution is no longer limited
to the educational events we host. It now belongs to you—and
to everyone you are moved to share it with.

In picking up this book, you have joined us in our

mission to ensure that Oregon's African American history is not forgotten but is instead resurrected, preserved, and widely disseminated. Welcome to the work that is our passion.

Introduction

Piecing together a history of a time, a place, or a people is not easy: the past is an elusive target. In our effort to learn about those who have gone before and to bring the stories of their lives into the present, we necessarily follow a broken path: one that is often as faint and hard to follow as the 150-year-old wagon tracks along the Oregon Trail. The path may be strewn with fragments of diaries, letters, undated or only partially legible newspaper articles, or handwritten census entries impossible to decipher. We may find unlabeled photographs or records of business transactions revealing no context: Who was the buyer? The seller? If we are lucky, we may acquire the first-hand childhood memories of people who are now elderly. Or we may encounter stories that have passed through so many generations that we can never hope to verify them and must remain content to accept them as "local legend" or "family lore."

In addition to the challenge of recreating history in general, we encounter the difficulty involved in piecing together African American history. Unique obstacles stem from the story's origin: slavery. People were ruthlessly and routinely separated from parents, children, siblings, and other family members. They could be sold and resold, acquiring the name of a new owner and often being relocated to a new place—a different town, state, or territory. And after slavery was abolished at last, the prejudice and discrimination that remained in its wake meant that the affairs and accomplishments of black people were seldom chronicled in the media of the day;

on the contrary, such media often served to perpetuate prejudice.

All of these hurdles—from the dearth of information about early black pioneers to scraps of paper that only hinted at fascinating life stories—stood between our researchers and the possibility of constructing an exhaustive history. So instead we present the facts to you just as they came our way. And unfortunately, we must omit information we would dearly love to offer but could not uncover: Who, for example, was the first black graduate of Willamette University? We do not know.

Where we had several good sources to draw from, we have gone into detail: the regionally famous Holmes child custody lawsuit of 1852 is an example. At other times, virtually all we know is that a black man or woman lived in the area in the past. One Alfred Drake, for example, is buried at the Salem Pioneer Cemetery. Of him, we know only that he was born in 1822 and died in 1875 and is listed in cemetery records as a "laborer." But Mr. Drake was here, and in this book we acknowledge and honor the fact of his life.

Similarly, some of the photographs we obtained pose more questions than they answer. The first few photographs in the gallery, starting on p. 223, are from the same collection—that of a Salem photographer who made portraits of several black citizens. We are fortunate that he sometimes labeled his photographs with his subjects' names and dated them, for now we know this much, but we are left to wonder about their lives: How did they earn a living? How were they regarded in the community? What were their talents, their strengths, their contributions? What troubles befell them? What personal resources did they draw upon to survive in an atmosphere of open and explicit anti-black sentiments and policies, even threats? Their elegant portraits may offer clues to their character, but in most cases, no further record of their lives has been found. We include their images despite the incompleteness of their stories. These individuals were here. They lived in the Salem area, and they rightfully belong to its history.

As you will learn in these pages, from the age of the wagon trains to the civil rights movement and into more recent times, the Salem area was often an inhospitable place for African Americans to settle. But settle they have, despite prejudice and discrimination, both overt and subtle. Although we lack a complete accounting of their lives, we know the difficulties and hostility they encountered, and we can imagine the qualities they must have possessed. Courage, determination, tenacity. A sense of resolve. Probably no small measure of stubbornness.

In a single word, perseverance. In persevering, the African American citizens of Oregon's Marion and Polk counties have moved the communities in which they lived ever forward toward full acceptance and recognition of their contributions. In this book we chronicle some of their steps along the way.

Note: Throughout this book, you will find boxed text
providing information on events outside
Marion and Polk counties for context. Those taking place
elsewhere in Oregon are indicated by an Oregon flag.
An American flag marks national events.

1

Life in a Peculiar Paradise: the Nineteenth Century

Being one of the "Poor Whites" from a slave state I can speak with some authority for that class—Many of those people hated slavery, but a much larger number of them hated free negroes worse even than slaves.

—Jesse Applegate[1]

We begin the first chapter of this book with an explanation of its title.

In the American South of the nineteenth century, the term "peculiar institution" served as a euphemism for slavery. Elizabeth McLagan folded the term into the title of her important 1980 book, *A Peculiar Paradise: A History of Blacks in Oregon, 1788–1940,* and it is an apt description of early African American experience in the state. From the beginning of white settlement, there was ample and open hostility toward blacks, as you will see. But compared to the horrific conditions slaves were enduring in the South, Oregon was indeed a relative paradise.

In chapter 2, we will introduce you to some of the first African Americans to arrive in Marion and Polk counties in the nineteenth century. In this chapter we will put the climate they faced in context, providing relevant information on territorial, state, and national events during this period.

The Oregon Country

Black people have a longer history in Oregon than might be realized. There is speculation that the first non-Indian to live here came ashore after a shipwreck at Nehalem in the late eighteenth century. This black man's name hasn't come down to us, but Native American legend says that the

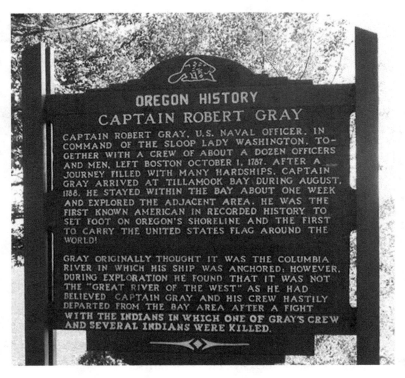

A historical marker on Highway 101 in Tillamook County commemorating the encounter between sailors and local Indians in which Marcus Lopius was killed

Tillamook tribe accepted him. He taught them how to render the metal parts of the ship into knives and married a woman of the tribe. An African named Marcus Lopius (or Lopez) was a crew member of the ship *Lady Washington* and landed at Tillamook on August 14, 1788; when the sailors got into a fight with local Indians he was abandoned by his shipmates, who last saw him being stabbed.[2] The Lewis and Clark expedition of 1803 included York, William Clark's slave. On the journey he had freedom and responsibilities equal to those of the

Winslow, Saules, and the Cockstock Incident

An event that blended hostility to blacks with fear of Native Americans contributed to the passage of Oregon's exclusion laws.

George Winslow, an African American, came to Oregon from California in 1834. In 1843 he was living and farming near Oregon City. He needed to clear some of his land and made an agreement with a local Wasco Indian named Cockstock: Cockstock would clear the land, and Winslow would give him a horse as payment. However, before the work was done, Winslow sold the horse and his farm to another black man, James D. Saules. Cockstock completed the work and asked Saules for the horse, but Saules refused. Angry, Cockstock stole the horse. The local Indian sub-agent, Elijah White, made him return the animal, and Cockstock swore revenge against Winslow and Saules, threatening them both over a period of several months.

After White tried without success to capture Cockstock in the winter of 1844, the Indian and five companions appeared at Oregon City. Fighting broke out; Cockstock and two local white men were killed. Sub-agent White prevented Wasco retaliation by compensating Cockstock's widow, but the incident raised white fear of attacks by local Indians. A charge against Saules helped poison the atmosphere further by bringing up the fear of Indians and blacks uniting against whites: during an argument with a white settler, Saules was alleged to have threatened to "incense the Indians" against the white man.[3]

Consequence of the Lash Law: A Black Man of Means Heads North

George Washington Bush, a black man of some wealth, traveled west on the Oregon Trail in 1844. One of Bush's fellow travelers, John Minto, wrote about Bush in his diary. He described a conversation in which Bush indicated he was concerned about how he would be treated in the Oregon Country: "He told me that he should watch, when we got to Oregon, what usage was awarded to people of color, and if he could not have a free man's rights he would seek the protection of the Mexican government in California or New Mexico."

The party stopped in The Dalles, and Minto rode ahead to Fort Vancouver for supplies. He returned with word of the infamous "lash law." At this news, Bush and a group of others broke with the train and—contrary to his initial plan to head south—pushed north across the Columbia River.

He became a successful farmer in what is now called Bush Prairie (near Olympia), famous for his generosity. But in 1853, the Donation Land Act in the newly formed Washington Territory forbade him ownership of the land he had settled because he was black. His neighbors repaid his good deeds by successfully petitioning Congress to pass a special law letting him keep his land.[4]

(continued on next page)

There has been considerable confusion stemming from multiple black men named Washington during this period of early settlement. A February 22, 1976, article in Northwest Magazine *incorrectly identified George Washington Bush as the man who founded the town of Centralia, Washington. However, a quick stop at the City of Centralia's website shows that the founder's name was simply George Washington. To make matters even more interesting, an entirely different George Washington, one who remained in Oregon, is buried at the Salem Pioneer Cemetery (see p. 121).*

white explorers. He was noted for his skill in scouting, hunting, and medicine. And at a time when slaves were forbidden to use weapons, York carried a firearm and shot game. His life after returning east fades into obscurity, and stories about him range from his dying a slave to escaping from slavery and spending the rest of his days with the Crow people of Wyoming.[5]

Jim Beckwourth, while not known to have traveled in Oregon, was one of several black mountain men who explored the Oregon/California region; Beckwourth Pass in California northwest of Reno is named for him. Other early black explorers known to have come to Oregon include Jacob Dodson, who as part of the Frémont expedition traveled down the eastern Cascades from Fort Vancouver to Klamath Falls,[6] and Moses Harris, who is profiled in chapter 2.

In the earliest days of white settlement, the United States and Great Britain both claimed control over what would become Oregon Territory. In 1846, the two powers signed the

Oregon Treaty, and what is now the state of Oregon became an American possession. Several years earlier in 1841, settlers had begun meeting in Champoeg, now a ghost town located a few miles north of present-day Salem. Their initial aim was to determine whether to create a provisional government. In 1843, they voted to do so.

In 1844, they turned their attention to the issue of slavery.

Many of these white settlers had come to the Oregon Country from states with harshly racist laws: Missouri and Ohio denied voting rights to free blacks and restricted their right to testify in court; Illinois and Indiana also had exclusion laws forbidding their presence in those states. The United States was undergoing a long series of crises over race that would culminate in the Civil War, and whites moving thousands of miles west to Oregon may have hoped to avoid the issue of race altogether by simply keeping black people— slave or free—out. The presence of slaves meant the possibility of a slave revolt; the presence of free blacks meant possible economic competition.[7] There was also fear that blacks would unite with Indians and attack white settlers.

To address all of these fears, the Oregon Country's provisional government passed "An Act in regard to Slavery and Free Negroes and Mulattoes" in 1844. Section 1 declared "That slavery and involuntary servitude shall be forever prohibited in Oregon." Sections 2 and 3 stipulated that slave holders had three years to "remove them out of the country" and if they failed to do so, they had to set them free. Black children could stay until they reached eighteen, but free blacks over that age had to leave within two years if male and three years if female. The penalty for breaking the law by remaining in the territory was at first a violent one: whipping. The offender would "receive upon his or her bare back not less than twenty nor more than thirty-nine stripes, to be inflicted by the constable of the proper county." If the person did not leave, six months later the punishment would be repeated, and again if the law was still not obeyed. It became known as the "lash law." However, shortly after its passage there were objections to its cruelty and the law was never enforced. The penalty was changed to forced labor: virtual slavery followed by expulsion. This law was to take effect in 1846 but was repealed in 1845.[8]

The 1845 Organic Code excluded nonwhites from voting:

> Sec. 10. Every free male descendant of a white man, inhabitant of this territory, of the age of twenty-one years and upwards, who shall have been an inhabitant of this territory at the time of its organization, shall be entitled to vote at the election of officers, civil and military, and be eligible to any office in the territory...[9]

The Oregon Territory

In 1848, the provisional government gave way to a territorial legislature, which passed a new exclusion law in 1849 again forbidding new black settlement but now permitting blacks who lived in the territory to remain.

The 1849 exclusion act met some resistance in the form of white Oregonians supporting their black neighbors and opposing the imposition of the law. For example, in 1851, 211 Portland residents signed a petition asking the legislature to exempt Abner Hunt Francis and his brother O. B., a merchant in the city:

> We the undersigned citizens of the Territory of Oregon, in view of an existing law passed ... in September of 1849 prohibiting Negroes or Mulattoes from settling

in the Territory, beg leave to call your attention to the severity of this law, and the injustice often resulting from the enforcement of it. There are frequently coming into the Territory a class of men to whom this law will apply. They have proved themselves to be moral, industrious, and civil. ... We see and feel this injustice done them, by more unworthy and designing men lodging complaint against them under this law... We humbly ask your Honourable body, to repeal or so modify this law that all classes of honest and industrious men may have an equal chance.

The Francis petition went on to argue that the danger of blacks and Indians threatening a unified attack on whites had passed.

Another petition was presented in 1854 in support of the right of Morris Thomas, a Portland resident. (See illustration, p. 11.) This petition was rejected, but there is no record of these black citizens being expelled; the Francises apparently lived in Oregon until they left voluntarily in 1860.[10] The passage of the federal Donation Land Act in 1850 superseded an 1843 provisional government law allowing white settlers to claim 640 acres. White settlers were now guaranteed 320 acres, and their wives another 320 acres.[11]

The federal Fugitive Slave Law was also passed in 1850, stipulating that runaway slaves could be pursued in any state and returned to their owners (see sidebar, p. 12). The law was misnamed, however: it also applied to former slaves, no matter how long they had been free.[12]

An expression of anti-black sentiment at the time is found in a June 13, 1851, editorial by Asahel Bush, publisher of the influential *Oregon Statesman* newspaper, presumably referring

A bill submitted to the territorial legislature in 1854 requesting that Morris Thomas be allowed to stay in Oregon

to abolitionists or other supporters of equality. "Their assertions that Negroes are entitled to approach our polls, to sit in our courts, to places in our Legislature are not more rational than a demand upon them that they let all adult bulls vote at their polls, all capable goats enjoy a chance at their ermine, all asses (quadrupled) the privilege of running for their General Assemblies and all swine for their seats in Congress."

On August 20, 1851, a black businessman named Jacob Vanderpool was arrested. A white man had filed a complaint

The Fugitive Slave Law, 1850

The U.S. Constitution provided for the return of slaves to their owners; this was the origin of the first federal fugitive slave law, enacted in 1793.

Enforcement of the law deteriorated with time. Northern states abolished slavery; abolitionism grew stronger; slaves escaped from the U.S. with the help of the Underground Railroad; sympathetic juries refused to convict runaways. Northern states passed "personal liberty" laws to protect blacks from being kidnaped, and forbade the enforcement of the federal law.

A new law was passed as part of the Compromise of 1850, requiring all citizens to aid in returning slaves under threat of severe fines. A black person would be tried in federal court but had no legal right to testify on his or her behalf. An owner's word, even if the owner was not present at the trial, would be sufficient evidence to send the black person south.

Northerners saw this new law as a Southern attempt to make slavery the law of the land everywhere, and widely protested against it. Some Northern states passed new personal liberty laws. Some citizens rebelled. In Boston, the government had to call out a thousand troops to escort Anthony Burns as he was forced to board a ship for passage back to slavery in Virginia. A federal official in Pennsylvania ordered local Quakers to help him seize a runaway slave; a riot broke out and the Quakers were later prosecuted but acquitted.

Shortly before the Civil War began, the South claimed that Northern disobedience to the Fugitive Slave Law was a justification for secession. Congress repealed the law in 1864.[13]

against him on the grounds that he was breaking the 1849 exclusion law. At his trial five days later, three prosecution witnesses testified as to when Vanderpool had arrived in Oregon; their testimony was vague, but the next day Judge Thomas Nelson found him guilty and ordered him to leave.

Vanderpool was thus the first and only known African American to be expelled from Oregon, though commentary in a local newspaper expressed the hope that he would not be the last. Referring to George Winslow (see p. 5), it reads: "A notorious villain, who calls himself Winslow, has cursed this community with his presence for a number of years. All manner of crimes have been laid to his charge. We shall rejoice at his removal."[14]

Vanderpool's fate after the trial is unknown.

A side note: It has long been thought that the Vanderpool case took place in Salem. However, he actually owned a saloon, restaurant, and boarding house in Oregon City. The confusion apparently stems from reports that his businesses stood across the street from the *Oregon Statesman*, which has long been a Salem newspaper (since 1853) but which started up in 1851 in Oregon City, the territorial capital at the time.

Statehood

Oregon ratified its state constitution in November 1857. On the popular ballot with the constitution were two other referendum issues on which citizens were asked to vote.

As the territory was preparing for its constitutional convention that year, a struggle for power was already in play between Democrats and the newly formed Republican Party over whether Oregon would enter the Union as a free or slave state. The "Salem Clique" of powerful Oregon Democrats had as its mouthpiece the *Oregon Statesman*, edited by Asahel

Bush, a leader of the group. In the newspaper, George Williams, the judge who had ruled in favor of the Holmes family in their custody fight (see chapter 3), published an influential document that became known as the "Free State Letter." In it he expressed his simultaneous opposition to abolitionism and the expansion of slavery into Oregon. While accepting slavery where it was already in place, Williams opposed its expansion on economic grounds.

Williams wrote, "One free white man is worth two negro slaves in the cultivation of the soil. ... Negroes are naturally lazy and as slaves actuated by fear of the whip—are only interested in doing enough to avoid punishment." He also argued that slaves were too expensive to keep, and that Oregon's climate was unsuitable for those used to "the blazing sun of Africa," and maintained that slaves would be "perfect leeches upon the farmer during our long rainy winters." They would escape to Canada or California. They posed the danger of allying with Indians to attack whites. They could undercut white workers, who would leave Oregon for better wages. If Oregon became a slave state, he warned, "... our happiness and prosperity would be sacrificed to the miserable strife about negroes."

Further, he argued that the new state could not afford to antagonize the economically powerful and generally anti-slavery North: "Can Oregon, with her great claims, present and prospective, upon the government, afford to throw away the friendship of the North—the overruling power of the nation—for the sake of slavery?"[15]

Bush supported Williams. "We believe that the African is destined to be the servant and subordinate of the superior white race ... that the wisdom of man has not yet devised a system under which the negro is as well off as he is under that

The *Dred Scott* decision, 1857

Dred Scott was a Missouri slave who sued for his freedom, first in state court and then in the federal system. In March 1857, the U.S. Supreme Court upheld Scott's slavery and denied his right to citizenship. Anti-slavery Americans were outraged. This decision overturned the spirit of previous North-South compromises that purported to let states determine whether to be slave or free; it established a precedent by which it could allow slavery to expand into the territories — or anywhere — by judicial fiat.

As for Scott, the sons of his first owner bought emancipation for him and his family in May 1857. He got a job in a hotel in St. Louis and was a celebrity in that city. He died of tuberculosis in 1858.[16]

of American slavery. Still … our climate, soil, situation, population, &c., render it … an impossible institution in Oregon."[17]

Oregonians rejected slavery but approved including a new exclusion law in Oregon's Bill of Rights.

When Oregon's constitution was submitted to Congress for approval, some Northern legislators complained about the exclusion law. However, others saw it as a structured way to avoid bloodshed over racial issues and the spread of slavery. Thus, in February 1859, Oregon became the only state admitted to the Union with an exclusion law in its constitution.[18]

By 1860, African Americans were present in fourteen of the nineteen Oregon counties.[19] The 1860 census lists them holding a range of occupations including barber, laundress, farmer, mechanic, shinglemaker, shoemaker — and slave.[20]

The vote to approve the state constitution				
	Slavery		Free black residency	
	yes	no	yes	no
Statewide	3,215 (25.5%)	7,195 (74.6%)	1,081 (11.1%)	8,640 (88.9%)
Marion County	210 (16%)	1,099 (84%)	82 (6.8%)	1,142 (93.2%)
Polk County*	231 (32.3%)	484 (67.7%)	53 (8.3%)	584 (91.7%)

*Luckiamute Precinct voted for slavery, 38–29.[21]

Post–Civil War America and Oregon: Laws for and Against Equality

The racism that had been codified in the state constitution persisted into the later half of the nineteenth century, despite post–Civil War amendments to the United States Constitution designed to expand the liberties of black Americans.

The Thirteenth Amendment

The Thirteenth Amendment to the United States Constitution, banning slavery, passed the state legislature in 1865. Four Democratic members opposed it. Further indicating where they stood, they also voted against an expression of sympathy over the death of President Lincoln, and voted against notifying Secretary of State Seward that the legislature had passed the amendment.[22]

Anti-Miscegenation Legislation

White opposition to intermarriage has a long history nationwide. Fear of blacks achieving social equality with whites, and blacks and Indian uniting against whites, were strong motivations for laws against "race mixing."[23]

Oregon enacted an anti-miscegenation law in 1867 prohibiting intermarriage between whites and blacks, Chinese, Kanakas (Hawaiians), or any person having more than one-half Indian blood. The penalty for breaking the law (by those marrying or those performing the marriage ceremony) was three months to a year in prison.[24]

The Fourteenth Amendment

The Fourteenth Amendment to the U.S. Constitution, which was ratified in 1868, guarantees citizenship (overturning the *Dred Scott* decision), due process, and equal protection under the law. The state legislature passed it in 1866, but only by 25–22; when Democrats won a majority in the legislature in 1868, the result of what the *Oregonian* claimed was an influx of "rebel guerilla population," they repealed the state's endorsement of the amendment.[25] The *Oregonian's* response: "Oregon is out of the Union!"[26] The state legislature would not ratify the amendment for more than a hundred years, finally passing it in 1973.

The Fifteenth Amendment

The Fifteenth Amendment prohibits the denial of the right to vote based on a citizen's "race, color, or previous condition of servitude" (slavery). It was ratified in 1870. The state legislature rejected the amendment on the grounds of "the right of the state to regulate suffrage"; this was purely symbolic language because the amendment was the supreme law of the land. The amendment was passed in 1959.[27]

Post–Civil War Salem

We know little of the history of the African Americans in Marion and Polk counties in the immediate aftermath of the Civil War. However, records that are available shed some light on that time: they describe two celebrations and a campaign to educate the young.

Celebrating Emancipation

The anniversary of the Emancipation Proclamation became a cause for joyful gatherings among African Americans around the country. Thanks to a January 3, 1868, article in the *Salem Daily Record* titled "Emancipation Jubilee" we know a few details of one such celebration attended by people from Salem, Albany, and the surrounding area.

At least three names that have become familiar to us appear in the article. Presiding over the ceremonies was "A. Bales, a blacksmith," whom we know to be Alfred Bayless. "Wm. Johnson opened the meeting with an earnest prayer." And "the address by Dan Jones was brief, pertinent to the day, and in good taste. He also read the Emancipation Proclamation very well, and it was listened to with great attention." All three men were connected with Salem's "colored school" (see p. 20): Johnson was its director, and Bayless and Jones published a notice regarding expenses for its "Evening School" (see illustration, p. 21).

The reporting on the Emancipation Jubilee and the available information on Salem's colored school begin to compose a picture of active community leadership on the part of prominent African American citizens at that time.

The *Salem Daily Record* article also portrays a white population beginning to accept the black citizenry in its midst. The event was attended by both blacks and whites: "Many of our citizens of both political parties were present, and we doubt if there was one among them all who failed to respect this effort of colored citizens to show respect for the day from which they date the freedom of their race in this nation." The article describes the African Americans gathered as "a very respectable company of colored people" and notes that "[t]he exercises were conducted entirely by themselves." It goes on to say that after the ceremony, there was "a social dance and supper, at which a few persons only [presumably white] remained to protect them from any intrusion."

The writer attempted to capture the significance and emotional power of the celebration for the black citizens (including six who had been freed by the Proclamation) who took part:

> The scene at the singing of the Battle-Cry of Freedom—"Rally round the Flag, Boys,"—called out all the enthusiasm of the impulsive race. Every voice shouted it, hands were wildly waved toward the flag, which formed a principal ornament of the room, and there could not have been an unmoved heart in the audience.

Records remain of a subsequent celebration in 1870, in which George P. Riley of Portland spoke eloquently of black contributions to the nation, starting in the Revolution and continuing into the Civil War, where "negro regiments ... were loyal to our flag and true to the best principles of our Government, and still ready to die for liberty and union ..." Following the address, the participants enjoyed a "very elegant supper ... quite as bountiful and excellent as could be conveniently have been gotten up in this latitude."[28]

The Colored School: Little Central

During the 1860s, all Salem households, black and white, were assessed a property tax to pay for the education of the city's children. Despite being required to pay this tax, African American families were barred from sending their children to public schools. In 1861, one man, William P. Johnson, went so far as to offer a five-hundred-dollar scholarship for his daughter-in-law to attend one of the city's schools, but his offer was rejected.[29]

Johnson and other black Salem citizens decided to raise funds to start a school of their own. The "colored school" opened in March 1867, its students taught by Mrs. Rufus Mallory. An accounting of the first term's expenses appears in the September 16, 1867, *Salem Daily Record:*

> THE COLORED SCHOOL.—W. P. Johnson, director of the colored school, returns the following statement of the receipts and expenditures of that school for the last six months:
>
> | | |
> |---|---|
> | Collected from citizens, | $430.75 |
> | Disbursed— | |
> | Incidental expenses, fitting up and warming room, | $ 67.50 |
> | Rent of room, | 60.00 |
> | Tuition, | 300.00 |
> | Cash on hand, | 3.25 |
> | | $430.75 |
>
> Mr. Johnson, on behalf of the colored citizens of Salem, desires to return thanks to the friends of his people for the kindness and liberality manifested.

Salem's public schools ca. 1893; Central School is in the middle and Little Central (the colored school) is at middle right

NOTICE is given that the colored people of Salem expect to pay all the expenses of the Evening School now being held by them, without aid from other citizens.— No person is authorized to collect funds in our name.

A. BALES,
D. JONES

SALEM, Jan. 21, 1868.

A notice in the *Salem Daily Record* indicating that there were evening classes at the "colored school"

It is not clear where the first classes were held. That same year, a one-story, two-room building, known as "Little" Central, was erected adjacent to "Big" Central School at High and Marion streets to handle the overflow from the main school. In 1868, Little Central became Salem's "colored school." Both school buildings were in use until 1905, when the city's first high school was built on the grounds.

We have no record of who attended Salem's colored school, but we do know of some families who were in the area at the time. It is likely that Roxanna and Lon, the children of Robin and Polly Holmes, attended, as well as two of William Johnson's grandchildren, Mary Ann and Orrie. Johnson's adopted daughter, Rosetta (Bonter), may have attended as well.[30]

In this chapter we have seen some of the ways American racial dynamics played out in Oregon and, locally, in Marion and Polk counties over the century. The pre-statehood events described here set the stage for what the first blacks faced as they arrived on the early wagon trains—the subject of the next chapter.

Plessy vs. Ferguson
In its Plessy *decision of 1896, the U.S.*
Supreme Court declared racism in public
accommodations to be the law of the land.

   A group of Louisiana citizens, black and white,
challenged a state law that forced black people to ride in
separate railroad cars; the law stated that such accom-
modations must be "equal." Homer Plessy, who was
one-eighth black (qualifying as black under state law), sat
in a whites-only car and announced his racially mixed
ancestry, letting himself be arrested in an act of civil dis-
obedience. Local and state courts upheld the law, as did the
U.S. Supreme Court, basing its decision on the "separate
but equal" principle, which Southern states used as legal
justification for expanding segregation.

   Plessy *stood until 1954, when the* Brown vs. Board
decision was handed down (see sidebar on p. 147).[31]

2

West with the Wagon Trains

It has been proved upon this floor that slavery does exist in the Territory in several counties. There are some in Benton, Lane, Polk, Yamhill and I know not how many other counties.
—William Allen, Yamhill Democrat, in introducing his resolution to protect the rights of Oregon Territory slaveholders, 1857

No negroes or mulattos shall be allowed to accompany the expedition under any pretenses whatever.
—Oregon Emigration Society rules, April 1843[1]

For most Americans, the word "pioneer" conjures certain distinct images and impressions. We picture wagon trains, pulled by teams of horses, mules, or oxen, crossing the barren plains. We see women dressed in long-sleeved, ankle-length dresses with bonnets tied under the chin and men in sturdy trousers and heavy shirts and boots, wearing broad-brimmed hats.

If we peer under the brims of the bonnets and hats, the grimy, trail-worn faces probably share a single feature—they are all white.

This commonly accepted vision of the pioneer is likely a composite of clichéd images we have encountered through the years—portrayals in old Westerns, perhaps an illustration or two from an American history textbook—all depicting European settlers headed west, determined and hopeful, in search of a better life.

But this is not the whole story.

In the 1840s and 1850s, a number of African American slaves traveled with their owners to Oregon Territory. Some of them settled on land that falls within the boundaries of modern-day Marion and Polk counties. When the earliest wagon trains arrived, neither county existed; the land that would become

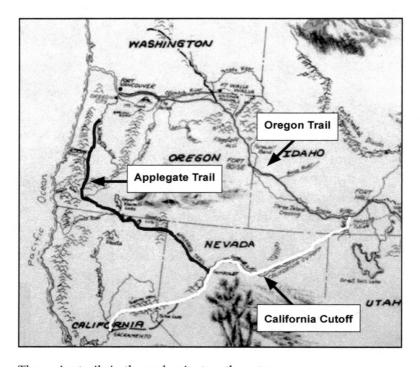

The major trails in the early nineteenth century

Marion County was part of a much larger Champoeg County, and Polk was in Yamhill County. There was flux in the borders for some time, but by 1860, the present-day borders of both Marion and Polk counties had been established.

As we have seen, slavery was technically illegal here during this early period, but there is no evidence that the new black settlers attained freedom upon crossing the border. On the contrary, in several instances the record leaves no doubt that they remained slaves for some time.

Here we chronicle some of the very first African

The Applegate Trail

In 1846, a small party from Dallas in present-day Polk County that included Jesse Applegate and his brother Lindsay surveyed a trail between the Willamette Valley and Fort Hall, near present-day Pocatello, Idaho. Their aim was to find an easier route for settlers than the more northerly Oregon Trail that followed the Columbia River.[2]

The Applegate Trail stretched five hundred miles. It was passable between May and October, and those who traveled it averaged fifteen miles a day.[3]

Americans to settle in the Salem area, many of whom were children when they arrived. We have chosen to list all who are known to us no matter how scant the surviving information about them may be.

But the first person we portray in our account of the wagon trains never lived in the area, as far as we know. We include him in this chapter because he was a pivotal character who guided wagon trains into the Oregon Territory and along the Applegate Trail, which wended its way through Polk County.[4] It is possible that some of the first black settlers would not have arrived safely without his expert help.

Moses Harris

Moses Harris is one of the best-known African Americans ever to travel to the Oregon Territory, and one of the first. Also known as "Black Harris" and "The Black Squire," he is said to have been born around 1800. Exactly where is unclear: one account places him in Union County, South Carolina, another somewhere in Kentucky.[5]

The importance of Harris to the area's history is underscored in an article titled "Black Harris and the Oregon Trail." In it, Thomas James Martin writes:

> ... Moses Harris was one of the foremost of the early western explorers and wagon train guides, a true free spirit who deserves more recognition for the part he played in settling the West.[6]

The adventurous Harris originally came west to help build forts and to do fur trapping. By 1822, he had traveled as far west as Yellowstone.[7] During his years as a trapper, he piloted supplies to fur traders and gained invaluable knowledge about wilderness survival. This positioned him well for the work he is better known for today: shepherding the wagon trains that brought settlers west on the Oregon Trail.

By the 1840s the fur trade had dwindled, so Harris began working as a guide for missionaries and settlers. At least three immigrating parties that we know of arrived under his guidance: the Whitman-Spalding party in 1836 and a large wagon train in 1844 that included the Bush, Holmes, and Ford parties. His skills were such that he effected at least two rescues:

> In 1845, Harris was in The Dalles when Stephen Meek stumbled into town after having gotten a wagon train lost trying to cross the high desert. Harris was the only person willing to help, and after bargaining for supplies from local Indians, he led the surviving members of Meek's party to safety at The Dalles.
>
> Harris later helped rescue a group stranded on the

Applegate Trail in southern Oregon, and he participated in efforts to explore the Cascade Mountain[s] in
search of a route better than the Barlow Road.

It is rare that we are afforded the luxury of insight into the
personalities of early black pioneers, but Harris's gregarious
character emerges from at least two sources. In 1844, a friend
named James Clyman wrote a mock epitaph for Harris:

> Here lies the bones of old Black Harris
> who often traveled beyond the far west
> and for the freedom of Equal rights
> he crossed the snowy mountain heights
> He was a free and easy kind of soul
> especially with a Belly full.[8]

In *Peculiar Paradise* we not only learn something of his de-
meanor but also find a physical description, contributed by
the artist who painted his portrait, Alfred Jacob Miller.

> This Black Harris always created a sensation at the
> camp fire, being a capital *raconteur,* and having had
> as many perilous adventures as any man probably
> in the mountains. He was of wiry form, made up of
> bone and muscle, with a face apparently composed of
> tan leather and ship cord, finished off with a peculiar
> blue-black tint, as if gunpowder had been burnt into
> his face.

Despite this description, there is still controversy over
whether Harris was actually a black man. After reviewing
all the sources available, we find the word "black" occurring

with sufficient frequency that we conclude he was indeed African American. We also have his own words on the subject (in a story told by fellow mountain man Jim Bridger): "Well, he sat down to dinner one day in a tavern, and a lady says to him, 'Well, Mister Harris, I hear you're a great trav'ler.' 'Trav'ler, marm,' says Black Harris, 'this nigger's no trav'ler; I ar a trapper, marm, a mountain-man, wagn!'"[9] No white man of that era was likely to describe himself that way.

Moses Harris died of cholera in 1849, in Independence, Missouri.[10]

Jane Bennett

Jane is believed to have arrived in 1844, traveling from Independence, Missouri, on a wagon train captained by Nathaniel Ford (see chapter 3 for more about Ford).[11] The train was guided by none other than Moses Harris. Jane was about eight years old when she first set foot in Oregon Territory and was the slave of Charles H. Bennett. Jane does not appear on wagon train records—and for that matter, neither does Charles's wife, Mary—but we find both of them listed in the Bennett household in the Marion County census of 1850. By the 1860 census, Jane's name has disappeared.

Jackson "Jack" Bonter

Jackson Bonter, a "pioneer Salem resident," was born in Kentucky in 1833.[12] He arrived in Oregon around 1855 and was a painter by trade.

In 1865 Jack married Mary Parks, a younger woman from Missouri. The officiating pastor at their wedding was Obed Dickinson of the Congregationalist Church (see chapter 5). The couple had three children: William, George, and Rosetta.

The gravestone of Rosetta Bonter
Johnson

Sadly, Mary died of "consumption" (tuberculosis) just a
few short years after their marriage, in 1870. International Order of Oddfellows research places her at age twenty-three at
the time of her death; this age conflicts somewhat with her
obituary:

Mary Bonter (colored) 20 years of age. She leaves three children. The funeral was numerously attended by friends and relatives, on Tuesday March 1st.[13]

In January 1872, W. P. (William) Johnson and his wife, Elizabeth, petitioned the Marion County Commissioners to allow them to adopt Bonter's young daughter, Rosetta. William, an African American man from North Carolina, was about fifty years old at the time and, like Jack, made his living as a painter. Elizabeth's occupation was "housekeeper."[14]

Jack Bonter also filed an affidavit with the court at this time, stating that he was Rosetta's father and that he wanted the Johnsons to adopt his daughter. We do not know why he desired this: Had it simply proved too much for him to raise three children on his own? Did he think the Johnsons could provide a better home for her? The latter could well have been the reason, as the 1870 census shows the Johnsons possessing real estate worth $4,000 and personal property worth $500. This was a very handsome estate for the time, and that fact alone is tantalizing: how did this African American couple, occupations painter and housekeeper, come to own such wealth?

It is possible that Jack Bonter never remarried: he is listed as a widower when he reappears in both the 1900 and 1910 Marion County censuses. In 1910, the aging Jackson Bonter's occupation had shifted from painter to "odd jobs." He lived into his eighties, dying in 1915. "Many friends" attended his funeral.[15]

Jack and Mary's son William died in 1877 at the age of nine years, ten months. His sister, Rosetta Johnson, died in 1889. No obituaries of either have been located.

George may have been the only child of Jackson Bonter

to survive well into adulthood. A George Bonter appears in a Multnomah County 1920 census—the only black Bonter found in Oregon at that time. He was a forty-eight-year-old repairman at a garage and a renter in Portland, married to Adeline Bonter, also forty-eight.

Jack, Mary, and William Bonter are all buried at the Salem Pioneer Cemetery, as are Mary's twin brother, Marion Parks, and William and Rosetta Johnson. A Nancy Williams, née Bonter, and her husband Jesse are also interred at the cemetery. One L. Bonter is also buried there, gender and occupation unknown; all the information we have about this member of the Bonter clan is that he or she was born about 1838 and died in July 1858.

Rachel Belden Brooks

In her 1927 publication, *Book of Remembrance of Marion County, Oregon, Pioneers, 1840–1860,* Sarah Hunt Steeves describes Rachel Belden Brooks as "the first known Marion County slave woman."[16] She was the property of Daniel Delaney and traveled to Oregon with him by wagon train in 1843. Before leaving Tennessee, Delaney sold off most of his slaves, but he purchased Rachel, "a strong young negro girl of about eighteen," from her former owner (named Belden) for a thousand dollars, in part to care for an ailing Mrs. Delaney on the journey west.

Rachel continued to live with the Delaneys until after the Civil War, working in the fields, the gardens, and the house and nursing Mrs. Delaney.

Rachel had two sons before marriage, Noah Newman and Jack. We assume they were Delaney's. This would be a reasonable conclusion to draw in any case, as it was not unusual for slave owners to father children by their slaves, but there is

Mulatto

The word "mulatto" appearing on early census records is an outdated term for a person who is of mixed European and African descent. During slavery, it was not uncommon for slave owners to father children by their slaves. These children generally inherited the slave status of their mothers.[17]

further evidence: In 1866 after Delaney's death, Rachel—then Rachel Brooks—sued his estate for a thousand dollars on behalf of herself and Noah Newman. We find no explicit description of the nature of the claim, but Delaney was a wealthy man, and it is likely Rachel was at least in part pursuing her son's inheritance. She won the suit, as evidenced in a settlement receipt her lawyers wrote. Phrased in the legalese of the time, the document begins:

> Received of William Delany Administrator of the estate of Daniel Delany as discussed the sum of one thousand dollars in full of all demands and claims of whatever kind or character due or to become due or claimed by us from the estate of said deceased either on account of the undersigned Rachel Brooks or Nathan Brooks or either or both of us and of all claim or demand whatever of the said Rachel Brooks as well as for all and every claim or demand of one Noah Newman, minor of the said Rachel ...[18]

With this transaction, the former Rachel Belden received

from Delaney's estate the exact amount he had paid to purchase her twenty-three years earlier.

Rachel's first marriage was to a man we know only as "Trave," who died. Then, sometime after 1860, she married Nathan Brooks.[19] For a few years they lived on the farm of Daniel Waldo, who had come to Oregon on the same wagon train as the Delaneys.

The couple had at least two children, sons Samuel and Mansfield. By the 1870 census the Brookses had a household of their own: husband, wife, and three sons—Jack, Sam, and Mansfield. Noah Newman is missing from the 1870 record. We are left to wonder whether he had died or had perhaps struck off on his own with some of the settlement money; if he was still alive he would have been twenty-three.

At some point the family moved to Salem, where Rachel became a familiar figure known as "Aunt Rachel Brooks." She lived to the age of ninety, dying on October 12, 1910, from a hemorrhage of the lungs. She is buried at the City View Cemetery in Salem.

A side note: Census listings of Rachel are much more complete than others we have found in our research of early pioneers, and they offer a good example of the inaccuracies in these old records. While she appears in every count from 1850 through 1910, estimates of her age vary widely. For example, she ages only four years between 1850 and 1860—from twenty-two to twenty-six—while from 1900 to 1910 she advances from age seventy-one to ninety-six.

Son Samuel surfaces in a 1930 article in the *Statesman Journal,* which relates that he worked for a sawmill for many years: "He hauled enough slab wood in his time to cover all Salem several acre feet deep."[20] He is buried at the Salem Pioneer Cemetery.

Rachel's 1910 obituary, entitled "Death Comes to Mrs. Brooks: Historical Character Dies in Salem at the Age of Ninety," describes her as "a well-known character" and "a woman of great industry and energy." The obituary states that she had been Delaney's slave, and it also asserts, peculiarly, that during that time she was considered "the pet of the family." Finally, the obituary perpetuates a mystery, reporting that she claimed to know precisely where on Daniel Delaney's homestead his elusive treasure was buried (see chapter 4 for more on the Delaney treasure).[21]

According to Steeves:

> Those who knew her best say of this slave woman, who knew nothing but hard work all her life, that all through her privations and the hardships she endured, she did not complain and was always kind.

"Ed"

The 1850 Andrew County, Missouri, slave schedule gives us one of two brief glimpses into the life of "Ed," slave of Benjamin Stanton. He was thirty-five years old that year, and beside his name, in the column listing race, is an "M" indicating mulatto. A very short narrative description of Ed is found in Steeves' *Book of Remembrance.* Here we learn that Stanton and Ed came to Oregon in 1853, and we get this account of Ed's role in the family:

> This old negro was very faithful to "Mars" Stanton and when freed with all other slaves he would not leave his master. It was one of his duties to be the fam-

ily cook, thus relieving Mrs. Stanton of much of the drudgery so common to the pioneer wife and mother.

Robin and Polly Holmes

Robin and Polly Holmes were slaves of Nathaniel Ford. They came to the Oregon Country in 1844 with their three children, Harriet, Celi Ann, and Jennie (or Mary Jane). Later in the book, we will discuss the Holmes family in some detail as we relate the story of Robin's lawsuit to gain custody of his children from Ford.

Rose Jackson

> … in 1850, a black woman, Rose Allen, rode to Oregon hidden in a large box. The white family with whom she traveled feared the uncertainty of her status in the western territories and allowed her to emerge only at night.[22]

Rose Jackson came to Oregon in 1850, the slave of Dr. William Richardson Allen. "The box story," as it has come to be known, has its origin in a pamphlet published by the Clackamas County Historical Society in 1962. As the story goes, Dr. Allen was well aware of the region's exclusion laws, and rather than run afoul of them, he planned to leave Rose behind. Rose, however, pleaded to accompany the family, and she had the support of Allen's daughters. Dr. Allen relented, and the family settled on a solution: they would smuggle Rose the entire length of the Oregon Trail in a wooden box drilled with ventilation holes. She would only be allowed to come out at night.

The box story is likely based in family lore, and we could find no corroborating evidence of it. If the kernel of the story is true—that the family at times hid Rose in a box as they journeyed west—it is highly improbable that she spent every day of the months-long journey in it. She was, after all, a slave; her job was to provide labor for her owner. Given the extremely hard work the tortuous journey entailed, it is difficult to imagine a slave would be allowed to sit it out, no matter how uncomfortably she rested. We will likely never solve the mystery of the wooden box, but one possibility is that Rose was confined to it when the Allens thought they were in some danger of losing her.

Rose was credited with saving the family much misery during their first winter in Oregon. Dr. Allen died shortly after the party arrived in the territory, and all members of the household had to find employment. William's wife, Martha Ann, found work as a seamstress, making roughly two dollars a day. Working as a laundress, Rose brought in as much as twelve dollars a day.[23] While she was technically free when she entered Oregon, as was any slave entering after the 1844 decision of the provisional government banning slavery, all her earnings went to support the Allen family. As was the case for most African Americans in the Oregon Territory, Rose was free only in theory.

Rose Allen became Rose Jackson when she married John Jackson, a groom for stagecoach horses in Canemah, an early settlement within present-day Oregon City. Rose and John moved to Waldo Hills in Marion County, where they raised their two children, Rose and Charles.[24]

In 1939, Mrs. Clyde B. Huntley of Portland, granddaughter of Martha Ann Barlow (Dr. Allen's wife remarried after he died), was interviewed as part of a Work Progress Administration project to capture early Oregon history. Her memories of Rose were not kind, reflecting racist sentiment she clearly felt comfortable expressing at the time. In describing life in the Southern Colonial home her family lived in, she adds:

> And no little glamour was added to all this by the presence of the two darkies grandmother had brought with her from the south, Old Rose and Peter, who stayed with her to the end. I was always horror-stricken at the sight of mother kissing Ol' Rose, who had nursed her from babyhood, but whose black skin was too alien to me for such affectionate demonstration.

This interview offers the only mention of another slave in the Allen household: Peter.

Travis Johnson

Philip Glover was born to parents who owned a large amount of land and numerous slaves. In Steeves' book we learn that Glover "joined the great caravan pushing westward to Oregon in 1849, taking with him his colored folks, among whom was a negro named 'Trav.'"

Travis was an expert ox driver—a skill that no doubt proved invaluable on the arduous trek west. When they arrived in Oregon, Glover hired Trav out as a driver and kept the proceeds from Trav's labor for himself. Travis is also described as an expert horseman and lover of animals. In fact, it seems animals were his life's work. He kept hounds and was called upon to use them to rid settlers of wild animals disturbing their flocks. And, according to Steeves, "he was often heard to say that he liked to hear the baying of his dogs better than the music of a piano."

The people of Marion County came to refer to Travis as "Old Trav." He journeyed around the region regularly, attending fairs with his animals and gathering news along the way. A reliable source of gossip, he was always made welcome despite a reportedly disheveled appearance.

When Travis came to Oregon with Glover, he was severed from his wife and children, who belonged to another man back in Missouri. After he "obtained" his own freedom (how or when this happened, we do not learn from the Steeves account) and was able to put some money aside, he struggled to purchase his family's freedom and bring them to Oregon. Though he spent much time and money trying to locate them, he was never able to. He died without an heir and was buried at Abiqua Creek in Marion County, northeast of Salem.

Maria Linville and "Johnson"

An article in the May 26, 1926, edition of the *Oregon Journal* captures the memories of Mrs. A. J. Richardson, daughter of Harrison Linville, the first Polk County judge. The Linvilles arrived in Oregon via the Applegate Trail in 1846 when Mrs. Richardson was an infant (born Hanna Jane).[25] She recalls that the family of her grandfather Richard, who came west with Harrison's party, was so pro-slavery that any family member who married a non–slave owner was disinherited; he did this at least twice. Mrs. Richardson offers this story about Maria:

> Grandfather Linville brought two of his slaves with
> him. When Maria, one of the slaves, was 16 she began
> to buy her freedom from grandfather. He agreed that

if he took her to a state where it was illegal to hold slaves he would return the money to her. She had paid grandfather nearly enough to buy herself when they decided to come to Oregon. When they started across the plains they didn't know whether Oregon was to be a free or a slave state. Some of the Southerners had brought their slaves with them. They hadn't been in Oregon long till it was decided Oregon was to be a free state, so grandfather gave Maria her freedom and paid back the money she had paid him, as he had agreed. He also freed the man he had brought with him.

The male slave who traveled with Linville, arriving as a boy of seven, is referred to in one source as "Johnson."[26] A "Wm." Johnson is listed at age eleven in the 1850 Polk County census. (This may have been the W. P. Johnson who was involved in establishing the Colored School in 1867; he would have been twenty-eight.)

In 1847, Richard Linville willed to his son Harrison "all rights I may have in my two slaves called Maria and Johnson now in Oregon." Apparently, Linville didn't find the Oregon provisional government's 1844 ban on slavery convincing enough to make good on his promise to free Maria right away. If Richardson's account is true, it probably happened after the Oregon statehood vote in 1857.

Matilda McDaniel

Matilda arrived on an 1844 wagon train from St. Joseph, Missouri, the slave of Frances McDaniel (née Embree). Matilda had been given to Frances by her father.[27] Frances and her sons Elisha and Joshua appear on the 1844 wagon train records; neither Matilda nor any of Frances's other children are listed. But in a book titled *Rickreall: Coming to the Vale of the Rickreall* we find an account of "Mr. McDaniel" (Frances's eighteen-year-old son Joshua), who would stake his claim in Polk County after stopping for the winter in the Tualatin plains and sharing a cabin with another family.

> His mother, two sisters, four brothers and a black girl that they brought with them and himself, occupied one end of the little cabin. ... Here they spent their first winter in Oregon, having arrived about December 15. Hard pressed for enough to eat, they lived principally upon boiled wheat, parched wheat and peas for coffee, their only meat consisting of about ten pounds of pork and occasionally some wild game secured from the Indians.[28]

Matilda was about twelve when the party arrived in Oregon. Frances supposedly freed the girl before she left for Oregon, but several days later "Tilly" somehow caught up with the family and traveled with them. We find "Tilly" mentioned again as a "Negro girl who lived with Mrs. Frances McDaniel, two miles east of Rickreall."[29]

A few years after the family settled here, Frances married John Howell, and it is in the Marion County census that we pick up Matilda's trail again at age eighteen. She is part of the Howell household along with Frances and five children.

After the Howell children were grown, Matilda apparently married and moved to Salem.[30]

Edward Ross

Edward Ross was likely owned by James Campbell, a farmer born in Greenville, Kentucky, who settled in the Waldo Hills area. Both arrived on an 1846 wagon train. They are not listed together in the wagon train logs—Ross appears by himself, not as part of the Campbell party—but we find Edward in the James Campbell household in the 1850 county census, age seventeen. He does not appear again.[31]

John Scott

John Scott came to Oregon Territory with the Nathaniel Ford party in 1844. According to papers written by Pauline Burch, a descendant of Ford who had much to say about him and his slaves (some of which contradicts other, less rosy accounts of events), Scott "wanted to accompany him." She describes him as young and single at the time. He was to drive the ox team hauling the supply wagon for the Ford family.

Once settled in Marion County, he married "a young free negro," Maria Linville, whom we have already met.[32] The couple had a son they named George. All are listed in the Marion County January 1850 census, with John about twenty-two, Maria twenty-six, and George a year old. (This census record provides another good example of inaccuracies concerning age: an earlier source estimates Maria's age at between eleven and fifteen in 1844; she leaps ahead at least five years in the 1850 census, perhaps as many as nine.) John is recorded on the census as mulatto and Maria and George as black.

Later that year, Scott went to the gold fields of California with another of Ford's slaves, Robin Holmes, and Ford's son Mark. Robin was the only member of the Ford household to return alive. On their journey back to Oregon, a tortuous ocean voyage during which they drifted off course and passengers became ill, Scott, Mark, and two other men volunteered to go to shore in an open boat to get help. The boat capsized and Scott and Mark drowned.[33]

In a Polk County census taken in October 1850, we find John's wife, Maria, and son George living with the Holmes family.

Hannah and Eliza Thorp

Hannah and Eliza Thorp (sometimes spelled Tharp or Thorpe) came to the Oregon Country in 1844 as slaves of John Thorp, a farmer born in Kentucky. Though there will be some discrepancies in their ages in later records, Hannah is thought to have been about twenty-four and Eliza about ten at the time.[34] They settled near Independence in Polk County.[35] In an early record, Hannah is described as "Aunt Hannah, a negress" and Eliza as "a mulato girl."[36]

Hannah and Eliza Thorp's Polk County trail goes cold after 1850, but their story doesn't end there. There is a later Marion County connection.

Hannah Thorp was also Hannah Gorman, mother of Salem resident Hiram Gorman (see p. 92). Eliza Gorman was Hannah's daughter and Hiram's sister. Sometime during the 1850s, mother and daughter made their way south to Benton County. In 1857 and 1858, they bought three lots on Fourth Street in Corvallis and built a small home on one of them. In 1866, Eliza bought another lot on the same street.

Eliza died in July 1869 at the age of thirty. She was buried at Crystal Lake Cemetery in Corvallis. In her obituary, we learn that Eliza had been a member of the Methodist Episcopal Church for well over a decade, and we discover something of the esteem with which she and her mother were held in the community.

Her intelligence, modesty, kind and sympathetic disposition, consistent Christian life, and uniform courte-

Hannah and Eliza Gorman's modest home still stands on Fourth Street in Corvallis. It was recently purchased to save it from demolition with the goal of restoration.

ous behavior, has won the respect and confidence of the entire community. Herself and her aged mother, by industry and economy had built them a comfortable home, furnished it in good style, and surrounded it with fruit, flowers, and everything necessary to human comfort and happiness. They seemed to live only for each other, and to make others happy.

After Eliza's death, Hannah moved to Portland. We find her in the 1870 census at age sixty, occupation domestic, living in the household of J. H. Wilbur, a Methodist minister. By 1875, Hannah's son, Hiram, and his wife, Georgia Ann, owned all of Eliza and Hannah's Corvallis property. They sold it that year to Hannah, who in turn quickly sold it to a man named Peter Polly. Hannah then apparently moved to Linn County and may have purchased property there as well. 1880 finds her back in Corvallis living on Second Street in the same household as Nancy J. Cook, her former white neighbor. She is sixty-nine years old and listed as a boarder.[37]

We do not know exactly when Hannah returned to Salem, but we know she died there in 1888, and it is presumed that she was living with her son, Hiram, and his family at the time. Her body was brought back to Corvallis and buried next to her daughter in Crystal Lake Cemetery.

In an ironic twist, in 1908 the Grand Army of the Republic (GAR), an association of former Union Army soldiers, erected a monument to honor Union veterans of the Civil War. To make room for the monument, the GAR had to move just two burials to a new location: those of John Thorp's former slaves, Hannah and Eliza.[38]

America Waldo

Daniel Waldo was one of the earliest pioneers to arrive in Oregon, traveling here in 1843 with Jesse Applegate, after whom the Applegate Trail is named. Waldo brought several slaves with him and staked his claim east of Salem in what are now known as the Waldo Hills. His house and the adjoining slave quarters still stand—although barely—presently nestled among the vines of a sizeable wine-making operation.

It has long been thought that among Waldo's slaves were the mother of his child and the child herself, named America. But new information has come to light. U.S. Census records and the dates on her tombstone indicate that America was born June 2, 1844, in Missouri. She moved to Oregon later,

The gravemarkers of Eliza and Hannah Gorman at Crystal Lake
Cemetery in Corvallis

possibly with Daniel's brother Joseph in 1846, and joined the Waldo household.[39]

Waldo became a member of the 1844 legislature, and voted yea on the draconian "lash law."

America married Richard Bogle, an emigrant from the West Indies, on January 1, 1863, in Salem, the same day Lincoln signed the Emancipation Proclamation. The ceremony was conducted by Reverend Obed Dickinson, who also hosted the wedding reception, an affair that was attended by both blacks and whites. (For more on Dickinson, see chapter 5.) This mixing of the races provoked the outrage of Asahel Bush of the *Oregon Statesman,* and was so controversial for its time that the event was reported in newspapers as far away as San Francisco.[40]

The couple soon moved to Walla Walla, Washington, to escape the restrictions of Oregon's exclusion laws and became successful ranchers and prominent citizens. In fact, Richard was one of the founders of the Walla Walla Savings and Loan Association.[41]

Elizabeth Walker

We learn of Elizabeth (also known as Betsey) from Walter M. Walker, who came to Oregon in 1848 and was elected Polk County commissioner and justice of the peace in 1849. In 1853, he wrote the following to a friend:

> I left Pike County, Missouri on the 9th day of Apl, 1848 to look for a home on the west side of the Rocky mountains. Somewhere in the neighborhood of the Pacific Ocean, say in the Willamette Valley, with my little family, wife, one little daughter and one yellow girl ...[42]

The Waldo house, built in 1853 and still standing east of Salem

Another source has the Walker party arriving "accompanied by black child Elizabeth who was about ten years old."[43]

According to an oral history related by a descendant of Walker, "the Negro girl Betsey Interford sat in the wagon caring for the baby." During the journey, the family apparently hid her in the wagon. "Her black skin had interested the Indians so much that the Major feared they would try to kidnap her."

Elizabeth appears in the Walker household in the 1850 Polk County census. She was evidently a skilled cook: "The kettle always sang on the crane in the big kitchen fireplace. There Betsey cooked the fine dinners for which she was famous.

"Betsey stayed with the family until the girls were grown," the narrative continues. "Then she married a man of her own race and settled in Portland where Major Walker's grandchildren visited her ..."[44]

We have now met the first wave of African Americans who are known to have settled in Marion and Polk counties. In chapter 6, we introduce you to a few of the later nineteenth-century arrivals. But first, in the next three chapters we offer more in-depth stories about some of the people we have touched on so far.

3

Close-up:
The Holmes Case

I so held, that without some positive [legislation] establishing slavery here, it did not and could not exist in Oregon, and I awarded the colored people their freedom ...

R obin and Polly Holmes arrived in Oregon in
1844 as the property of a man named Nathaniel
Ford. In their mid-thirties at the time, they brought
with them their three children: Harriet, seven; Celi
Ann, four and a half; and Jennie, two and a half.

The Holmeses' life in Oregon began like that
of most other early black settlers described in this
book: they entered the territory as slaves, despite the
fact that Oregon was technically a free territory at
the time. But by 1850 the couple would be free, and
in 1852, eight years after their arrival, Robin would
begin an unprecedented legal battle to get custody of
his children from Ford.

Holmes vs. Ford

The *Holmes vs. Ford* case is well documented in Polk County court records, which offer a remarkable window into the
racial dynamics of the time: the precarious status of African
Americans in Oregon's early pioneer days; the courage and
perseverance Robin and his family exhibited in asserting their
rights; and the fact that white settlers were divided in their attitudes toward African Americans, with some being willing to
take up Robin's cause in a court of law.

According to Holmes's testimony in April 1853, Nathaniel
asked Robin to leave Missouri with him and journey to Oregon, telling him that "Oregon was a free country, that slavery

OrHi bb06958

The Ellendale house of Nathaniel Ford, who brought Robin Holmes and family as slaves from Missouri in 1844

did not exist there, and he did not think it ever would." In a sworn affidavit initialed with his mark, Robin informs the court of the plan he and Ford agreed to before commencing the journey: The Holmeses would help Ford "open a farm." Then, after they had completed this work, Ford would release them into what was called at the time "free negro" status.[1]

So the Holmes family joined the Ford party, and together they made the exhausting seven-month trek by wagon train. They arrived at The Dalles in November, and after a brief rest they headed on to their temporary destination: Oregon City.

From Oregon City, Ford and some of his fellow travelers set off on horseback for the Rickreall Valley (in present-day Polk County) to claim land. Ford bought three adjoining tracts, purchasing them from a squatter named Billy Doak for $25.[2] Then he rode back to Oregon City to make arrangements to construct dwellings on the land. According to Pauline Burch, a descendant of Ford, he left Robin and his family at Oregon City to look after Mrs. Ford and their daughters, taking with him as a building crew only his son, Mark, and another slave he had brought with him, a man we know only as "Scott."[3]

The crew built three cabins—one for the Ford family, one for the Holmes family, and one for Scott—and everyone settled into their new homes. Ford gave Scott and the Holmeses plots of ground on which to raise vegetables for sale, and this was how they subsisted—"with a good income," according to Burch—from 1845 to 1848.

In Ford's personal records, he maintains that those first few years were happy ones for everyone living on his land— blacks and whites alike. If any personal records of Robin or Polly had survived, they might contain a different conclusion about the parties' relative happiness: during those years Ford reneged on his promise to grant Robin and Polly their freedom. Finally, in 1849, Holmes's patience wore out, and he explicitly asked to be released from service.

This request was not granted until the following year. First, Ford insisted, Robin must journey to the gold fields of California. Robin made the trip and arrived back safely, apparently returning with $900 in gold of his own. Scott and Mark Ford, who traveled with him, were not so fortunate; both drowned on the return journey.[4]

The circumstances under which Ford at last granted Robin and Polly their freedom were at the heart of the subsequent lawsuit. Ford maintained that on March 1, 1850, he and Robin entered into an agreement: "Robin and his wife were to be and remain henceforth free—that they were to take their youngest child and keep it—And that this Respondent [Ford] were to keep all the rest of the said children together with one which has since died, and which was the oldest of the said family of children, and to hold them until they respectively became of age, according to the laws of the Territory, to wit the males twenty years of age and the females eighteen years of age. To hold them not as slaves, but as wards."[5]

Holmes maintained he had made no agreement of the kind. And thus the stage was set for *Robin Holmes v. Nathaniel Ford*.

Absent a legal ruling on the dispute that would not come for more than three years, Robin and Polly had no further choice in the matter of their children's custody. They left the Ford property and moved with their infant to Nesmith Mills (later renamed Ellendale, now a ghost town about two and half miles west of Dallas),[6] where Robin found employment.[7] Their four other children—Harriet, now age thirteen, Mary Jane, now eight and a half, James, five, and Roxanna, three— remained with Ford.

Robin Holmes's legal challenge formally commenced on April 16, 1852, with a writ of habeas corpus filed against Ford by one of Holmes's attorneys. It began: "You are hereby com- manded that you have the bodies of Jenny or Mary Jane Hol- mes, Roxanna Holmes and James Holmes, by you unlawfully detained." Before the case was decided, Holmes would have three attorneys representing him: O. C. Pratt, Joseph C. Wil- son, and A. G. P. Wood.[8]

The legal battle was contentious. Adding to his assertion that he and Holmes had made a deal allowing Ford to keep the children, Ford accused Holmes of being an inadequate parent, claiming he was "poor and ignorant and unfit to have the care, custody and bringing up of said children." He went on to further justify his claim on the children this way:

That this Respondent [Ford] has kept the said children

at a heavy expense when they were young and their services of very little or no value—and now since they have arrived at an age when their services will be of some consequence the Respondent insists that he has a right to retain said children ... as a part compensation and remuneration for the expenditures made in their behalf—[9]

So to Ford, there were three clear reasons he had the right to custody of Robin and Polly's children: he had made a deal with Holmes; Holmes was incapable of parenting his own children; and he, Ford, had earned the children's labor by feeding and clothing them.

Holmes took issue with each part of Ford's response to the writ in turn, first by insisting that he did not "make an agreement with said Respondent [Ford] or any one for him, by which said Respondent was to keep said minor children and be entitled to their services until they became of age or for any period of time, but on the contrary claimed that they should be then liberated and delivered to your petitioner [Holmes]." The affidavit goes on to state that since that day of alleged agreement in 1850, Robin had "ever since sought to obtain the custody and control of said children."

Holmes further asserted that it was Ford—not he—who was the poor guardian, and that Ford had not allowed Robin to see his children in more than two years. He claimed that Ford has not adequately fed and clothed the children, that he feared for their well-being, and that he believed it was Ford's intention to sell them into slavery, putting in jeopardy "their life, liberty and happiness." Might this echo from the Declaration of Independence tell us the real underlying argument, remarkable for its time, of Holmes's legal action—that freedom from tyranny applied not only to European settlers throwing off the yoke of a foreign power, but to African Americans resisting domestic tyranny?

Robin concluded his parenting argument by denying that he was "unfit by reason of his poverty and ignorance to have the care and custody of his own children." On the contrary, he argued, his "character for honesty, society and industry is good ..."[10]

Children for Sale?

In a document entered into the record that seems to have been included as evidence that Ford was a reasonable man, he tells the court that he had been advised to sell the family back to Missouri but chose not to do so. Holmes's response to this is illuminating:

> ... your petitioner [Holmes] does not know whether said Respondent [Ford] has ever been advised to take your petitioner and his family back to Missouri and sell them into slavery or not, but he does know and states the fact to be that Respondent has often threatened to do so, for the purpose of deterring your petitioner from seeking to obtain the custody and control of said children ...

Whether Ford received advice from someone else to sell the family or it was his own idea, it is irrefutable that he explored the prospect, and it appears that this was at least in part because his determination to keep the Holmes children had begun to cause him major headaches—difficulties he laid at the feet of abolitionists. On June 22, 1852, more than two years after their alleged agreement about the children's status, Ford wrote a letter to a friend in Missouri named James A. Shirley "asking that he satisfy one of Ford's old debts, so that Robin, his wife and the children, might be returned to Missouri under the Fugitive Slave Act, and sold there upon the block."[11] Ford writes (spelling from the original letter is reproduced here):

> You know I brought some negroes with me to this country which has proved a curse to me and my fambly. Scott died. Robin and his wife done verry well untill the spring of '50 when the abolitionists interfered — and the country is full of them — the interference was so great that I had to let them go. They have stoped in some six miles of me with a man who owns a mill [this may be a reference to Nesmith Mill, where Robin worked] and the abolitionists are so much about them that the negroes are continuly harrissing my fambly by attempts to slander them.
>
> Now my dear friend I wish you if you care to befriend me — though I am in a distant land, you know Crigler the sheriff had levyed an execution on the negroes and they were brought off to this country. I am of the opinion that the execution may be renewed as to send it here and take the negroes back to Missouri under the fugitive slave law. If so if you will have it attended to and appoint an agent here, ... I will pay all the expenses here and git all the evidence which is in my neighborhood. ... Robin and his wife are very likely — they have five likely children if you can make the arrangement you may make some 1500 to 2000$ out of them and do me a great favor.
>
> If the negroes can be taken under the fugitive law

I will make arrangements to send them to you in short
order ... if the case of the negroes can be attended to
it will releave me and my fambly of much trouble and
you may be benefitted by it.[12]

As the case progressed, Ford sought to back up his claim
of an agreement with Robin by soliciting testimony from then
General Joseph Lane. Lane, after whom Lane County, Oregon,
is named, was a vocal proponent of slavery. However, in an
interesting twist (and unfortunately for Ford), when it came
to written testimony under oath, Lane proved to have little
recollection about any discussions of the fate of the children.

The wheels of justice creaked slowly along. One reason
the case lingered, it is thought, was that no judges were ea-
ger to wade into a conflict where the Pandora's box of slavery
might be opened. Though Ford was not claiming the children
as slaves, using instead the term "wards," this difference in
semantics may not have been persuasive to judges facing the
prospect of having to decide such a controversial case.

Three judges heard the case at various stages but did not
rule: O. C. Pratt (who, interestingly, had filed the original writ
on behalf of Holmes), Cyrus Olney, and Thomas Nelson.[13]
It was not until George H. Williams, a free-soil (antislavery)
Democrat from Iowa, was assigned to the region that the case
was decided.[14] The date was July 13, 1853. In settling a dispute
that had raged for more than three years, Williams entered a
succinct paragraph into the record in a verdict issued at Dallas
in Polk County, which concluded:

... that the said Jenny or Mary Jane, James and Roxanna be and they are hereby awarded to the care and
custody of their parents Robin Holmes and his wife to

be and remain with them as their children as fully in
all respects as though they the said children had not
been in the custody of the said Ford ...

Williams also ordered Ford to pay all the costs of bringing
the case to trial and adjudicating it: a grand total of twenty-
one dollars and fifty cents.[15]

Years later in 1866, when the state legislature acted on the
Fourteenth Amendment of the Constitution, which expanded
the definition of citizenship to include African Americans and
effectively overruled the *Dred Scott* decision, Ford was a state
senator, then representing Umatilla County. The vote to ratify
the amendment passed in the senate 13 to 9. Ford was among
those voting nay.[16]

And so we see that Williams's written decision did not weigh
in on the practice of slavery—it sidestepped the issue entirely.
But later, in a 1901 article published in *Oregon Historical Quarterly,* he clearly revealed his thinking:

> Whether or not slave holders can carry their slaves
> into a territory and hold them there as property, has
> become a burning question, and my predecessors in
> office, for reasons best known to themselves, have de-
> clined to hear the case. ... I so held, that without some
> positive legislative [sic] establishing slavery here, it
> did not and could not exist in Oregon, and I awarded
> the colored people their freedom. ... So far as I know,
> this was the last effort made to hold slaves in Oregon
> by force of law. There were a great many pro-slavery

men in the territory, and this decision, of course, was very distasteful to them.[17]

After the Decision

The Holmes family moved to Salem (whether this occurred during the legal battle or after is unclear). There, Robin established a nursery, which was apparently quite successful. According to a 1952 article in the *Sunday Oregonian Magazine*, "Many fruit trees planted by Polk and Marion County horticulturists in the 1860s were raised by Robbin [sic]."[18]

Robin's and Polly's Deaths

On February 1, 1862, Robin wrote a will. By this time he referred to himself as Robert, wrote in his own hand, and signed his full name. In it he states that he is of sound mind but "of failing health of body." He appoints as his executor a Judge Boise of Marion County, asking him to take possession of his personal property "and my real property in North Salem" and with the proceeds to have him interred and his debts paid. If his personal property was not sufficient, he asked that Boise "dispose of my real estate in sufficient quantities" to pay all of his debts. Beyond this, he bequeathed each of his children the sum of five dollars and asked that everything that was left go to Polly. He is believed to be buried at the Salem Pioneer Cemetery, as he purchased Lot 202 for his family in 1862, the year of his death, and his son James and daughter Roxanna are buried there.

All we know of Polly's later years and death is that in 1870 she was in the State Insane Asylum[19] and that she died in Portland.

Following the Holmes Children

Mary Jane

Before the court case, Ford had already given Mary Jane Holmes to his daughter, the wife of one Dr. Boyle of Salem; she apparently remained on as part of the Boyle household even after the court decision.

In 1857, she was married at her parents' home to a man named Reuben, who had come to Oregon as the slave of Robert Shipley.[20] Shipley had promised Reuben he would free him upon their arrival in Oregon in exchange for driving their team of oxen to the territory. Unlike Ford, Shipley apparently kept his promise, and Reuben soon gained employment with a nearby farmer named Eldridge Hartless, who was quite well off. Reuben was able to save some money and eventually purchase a large farm for his family.

It is said that Ford was paid to release Mary Jane to her husband. The year they married was also the year of the *Dred Scott* decision, which opened all territories to slavery despite the preferences of their citizens. So technically, Ford would have been able to claim Mary Jane as his slave.

Accounts conflict concerning how and why Reuben paid Ford. One has it that Ford declared up front that Mary Jane was still his property and demanded a payment of $700. Another account has Reuben's white friends—without Ford's knowledge—convincing him he should pay Ford. Contrast this with the version that has Reuben paying off the sum over several years until his white friends learned what he had been doing and insisted he stop. The only common understanding is that, one way or another, Reuben had to purchase his wife.[21]

Mary Jane and Reuben went on to buy a ranch near Philomath, deeding three acres to a "Committee to establish

OrHi 89474

Mary Jane Holmes Shipley in 1924

a Cemetery" where blacks could be buried. Mary Jane and her family are now buried there, at Mount Union Cemetery. A commemorative stone at the entrance reads:

On may 11, 1861 Reuben and Mary Jane Holmes Shipley, former negro slaves, deeded from their farm purchased from Charles Bales donation land claim, the original plot for this cemetery. Buried in lot 10 are Reuben Shipley, Mary Jane Shipley Drake, Alfred

Mount Union Cemetery in Philomath

Drake, and the Shipley children, Ella, Wallace, Martha, William.

Lon Holmes

We have this account of Lon Holmes's death: "One day early in 1864, Polly came running to the Boyle home and said: 'Some men are hanging my Lon'. She said she had told them: 'If Mars [unintelligible] or Dr. Boyle was here you wouldn't dare do dat. I would settle you meself if I hadn't de grace of God in me heart.'" It seems that some gamblers had lost money and tried to accuse Lon of stealing it; they had ransacked Polly's home looking for it, Lon maintaining his innocence all the while. Dr. Boyle ran to the scene and was able to stop the hanging. But it was too late: Lon died of his injuries.[22]

❖

According to Pauline Burch, "The last recorded contact made by any of the Ford family with the family of Robin and Polly was a visit by Caroline Ford Burch to Mary Jane during her last illness, while she was in a Portland Nursing Home where she passed away at the age of 82 1/2 years."[23]

Two of the Holmes children—Roxanna and "Leonidas"— are buried at the Salem Pioneer Cemetery. His obituary in the *Weekly Oregon Statesman* of March 16, 1877, is brief: "Died—In Salem, March 10th, of consumption, Leonidas Holmes, colored." Yet he had nearly died seven years earlier, as a newspaper clipping reveals:

ALMOST DROWNED.—A colored boy named Leonidas Holmes came pretty near to being drowned yesterday. He was standing on the guards of the steamer Fannie Patton, when a young man who had been investing in "wet groceries" came up, and declaring that Leonidas was one of the best fellows in the world, gave him a playful shove which sent him spinning into the river. Being unable to swim, the boy sank twice before he could be rescued by the hands on the boat, who came promptly to the rescue.

Roxanna died at twenty-six, also of consumption, leaving behind her husband, Charles Miller. According to cemetery records, they had been married on December 27, 1865, by "O. Dickenson." (Rev. Obed Dickinson is the subject of chapter 5.)

4

Close-up:
The Murder of
Daniel Delaney

The boy Jack—a mullatto—was called. (Defense objected to his testifying on the ground that negroes could not under the law testify in a criminal trial where a white man was on trial. Objection over-ruled.)

In January 1865, one of Marion County's early white pioneers was murdered by two other white men—dressed in blackface. The dramatic story has no doubt been embellished in the retelling, but the basic facts can be found in transcripts from the ensuing trial.

Daniel Delaney Sr., by then in his seventies and known as "Uncle Daniel Delaney," lived virtually alone in the Waldo Hills in what is now the Turner area east of Salem. The only other residents of the house at the time were a black boy named Jack (believed to be Delaney's son by his slave Rachel Brooks—see p. 35) and a family dog. Delaney's wife, an invalid, was living nearby with son Daniel Jr. at the time.

Delaney had done well for himself in Oregon and had accumulated quite a sum of money. At a time when there were no banks, people often hid their cash on their property, and he was widely believed to have done this.

Enter one George Beale, a man who was well acquainted with Delaney and his wealth, having worked for him around his house and property. He knew that Delaney had recently made a great deal of money from a large cattle deal and noticed that Delaney kept a small keg near his bed.

Beale was anything but discreet about his desire to get his hands on Delaney's riches. He talked freely around town about the money he believed might be stored in that keg, so much so that he was warned to leave the old man alone.[1]

George Baker had just opened a saloon. Though he was relatively new in town, he and Beale had been acquainted for some years. Together they hatched a plot to rob Delaney, one that hinged on his reputation for being friendly to blacks.

The pair traveled to the Delaney homestead, Beale on foot and Baker on a horse. Upon arriving, figuring "Uncle Daniel" would be more willing to open his door to blacks in need of directions than whites, they stopped at a watering trough and darkened their faces with lampblack.

Once they had set the stage, Beale opened the gate, went up to the house, and knocked. Delaney opened the door and Beale asked for directions to Daniel Jr.'s house. Delaney came out onto the porch. Beale maneuvered him so that Baker had a clear shot, and Baker pulled the trigger.[2]

Shot, Delaney staggered back, then recognized Beale and said, "I know you, Beale, for God's sake, don't kill me. Spare my life and you may have all the money I have."

Beale is said to have answered, "Old man, dead men tell no tales." Then he, too, shot Delaney, this time between the eyes.[3]

The dog set up a commotion, so Beale shot him too. But he didn't realize that Jack was also inside. The boy grabbed the dog, ran back into the house, and bolted the door. The two men attempted to kick in the door, and Jack fled out the back. He hid in a woodpile all night while Beale and Baker ransacked the house. In the morning, when the boy was sure the men had left, he ran to Daniel Jr. and told him what had happened.

It is safe to say that Beale and Baker were not smart men. They began spending money around town and paying off debts with $20 gold coins. And according to a descendant of Beale who researched the story, Beale had asked two or three other men to rob Delaney before finally deciding to do it himself. It was just a matter of time before the pair would be caught.

They were free for a total of five days after the murder. According to testimony at the trial, during this time Beale claimed "it was the 'niggers' around here" who had committed the murder, adding that "there was getting to be too many d—d niggers around here anyhow."[4] But in addition to the circumstantial evidence of the duo's sudden spending spree, a hatband found at the trough matched Beale's hat—missing its band—to a tee, and both men were arrested.

They both eventually confessed, though each attempted to shift the blame to the other. They admitted to taking about $1,400 of what Delaney's sons estimated as a $70,000 fortune. (After the crime, the sons found about $24,000 of this upstairs in barrels of corn, and another $3,000 in the granary.)

Jack was the only eyewitness to the murder. At first, he was prevented from testifying at the trial because he was black. Court transcripts read: "The boy Jack—a mullatto—was called. (Defense objected to his testifying on the ground that negroes could not under the law testify in a criminal trial where a white man was on trial. Objection over-ruled.)" Then Jack was asked a few questions, such as whether he knew what a lie was and, bizarrely, what kind of place hell is. The defense then reargued against allowing Jack to testify, claiming that "the boy had not sufficient intelligence to take the oath." The judge sustained this new objection but later allowed his testimony.[5]

The two men were found guilty and were hanged in Salem on May 17, 1865, the first men to be hanged for murder in Marion County, and possibly in Oregon. Thousands of people traveled from surrounding counties to witness the double execution, which was held in downtown Salem near what is presently Pringle Creek Park.[6] Among the crowd were children, one of whom was fourteen-year-old T. T. Greer, who walked seven miles to view the spectacle. Greer would later become governor of Oregon and write about his revulsion at the scene.

Baker's family took his body, but no one claimed Beale's. In the end Daniel Waldo buried it in his family's cemetery. One account has it that Waldo did so because he was angry that local cemetery wardens refused to take responsibility for the burial; another gives the reason that Beale was an in-law of Mrs. Waldo. In any case, the cemetery where Beale is buried still sits on a knoll in a field about a half mile north of the old Waldo house.

What about the money Delaney's sons didn't find? According to a July 28, 1957, article in the *Oregon Statesman,* "From the time of Delaney's death till a few years ago, men have dug in various places on the farm looking for the money. They used divining rods, dowsing sticks, electronic instruments, and followed advice of clairvoyants ... [P]eople continued to dig in various places for years afterward." No one has ever reported finding the money.

In the foreground, the Waldo cemetery where George Beale is buried. In the distance, the Waldo house sits in a stand of trees.

5

Close-up: Obed Dickinson Battles Racism

It is true, we have no slavery in Oregon; but we have that which is equally wrong: a prejudice and a hatred of the oppressed race.[1]

The career of the Reverend Obed Dickinson gives us a focused view of white Oregon's attitude toward African Americans from the 1850s to the post–Civil War period. He was far ahead of his fellow whites in his thinking about black people, and paid a price for it.

Dickinson was born in Massachusetts in 1818 and graduated from Andover (Massachusetts) Seminary. He married Charlotte Humphrey in September 1852 and the couple sailed to Oregon two months later, taking residence in Salem under the sponsorship of the American Home Missionary Society. The First Congregational Church where he served as pastor was small and poor—four members and a dirt floor in its early days.

Oregon's population in 1860 was fifty-two thousand. Salem, the territory's capital, had a population of eleven hundred. Marion County's population was around seven thousand. The county's black population was very small (estimated at seventeen for that year). The white settlers in the area came in large part from the South as well as such border states as Missouri where slavery was legal, and they brought their attitudes and their politics with them. The Willamette Valley was a Democratic stronghold under the control of the Salem Clique, and Asahel Bush's *Oregon Statesman* had a powerful influence on local politics. Oregon had been divided on

The Rev. Obed Dickinson

the issue of whether the territory would enter the Union as a free or slave state, but with few exceptions, it was not divided on hostility to black people.

The Rev. Dickinson was such an exception. He belonged to the Congregational Association, which was antislavery, working to abolish the institution "in the way best for both the slave and master."[2] In 1859, it resolved not to allow preaching by slave owners or those in favor of slavery. This was directed at pro-Southern clergy: Southern Methodists affirmed "civil rights" (slaveholders' property) and Southern

Baptists had moved into the area and enjoyed better atten-
dance at their churches.[3]

Dickinson's church attracted black parishioners, perhaps
the first such white church in Oregon to do so.[4] Accompany-
ing Obed in his work, Charlotte opened the Dickinson home
to teach illiterate black women to read, leading classes every
evening for four women, plus "a fifth as often as her mistress
will allow."[5]

At the same time, the country was on the verge of civil
war. Even Bush's *Statesman* was alarmed: "The secession papers in Oregon are becoming every week more insolent and
abusive of the union and more emphatic in their advocacy of
Davis' confederacy ..."[6] However, his attitude was based on
the divisiveness of slavery as an issue, not its immorality, and
the importance of preserving the Union.

Around this time, Dickinson reported to the American
Home Missionary Society on his work and the response it was
eliciting. He had spoken out from the pulpit and person to
person, emphasizing equality and the evil of racism. For example, he once berated a white parishioner for her opposition
to black membership:

> The wife of our brother [the church's deacon, I. N. Gil-
> bert] came to me wishing to have a "separate" meet-
> ing on Sunday or some other day for the blacks to
> unite with the church. ... I told her Christ had given
> us no warrant for such distinctions ...[7]

On June 16 he preached a sermon based on the text, "In-
asmuch as ye have done it unto one of the least of these my
brethren, ye have done it unto me," decrying Salem's denial of

public education to black children while taxing blacks' property to pay for white schools.[8]

His white flock was not as receptive as he might have wished, especially at a time when he needed their financial support to complete the construction of a new church. This sermon created *"feelings."*

> A brother came to me next day and said, "That sermon will take away five hundred dollars from our Church Building. You had better wait till the church is finished before you preach on these exciting subjects." I said I must preach it, God says thou shalt not suffer sin upon thy neighbors.[9]

In his report, Dickinson also described the torture of a black boy accused of theft when a series of burglaries struck his parishioners:

> The husband of a cousin of our deacon (a southern man) lost money also. He laid it to a negro boy so ignorant that he hardly knew his right hand from his left, and to compel him to confess gathered a company and hung him till some supposed he was dead. For parts of three days an excited gang of men in our streets trod down all law and right—hanging chooking [sic] and whipping that poor boy. My whole soul was stirred within me. I condemned such actions ... yet many of our citizens being southern men, they were able to carry on their work so long. The boy was finally lodged in the jail and after two months tried and acquitted as an innocent boy ...[10]

"I am stubborn ..." Dickinson stuck to his insistence on admitting black people to the congregation and campaigning for justice for Salem's black citizens. He was able to persuade the congregation to accept black members.[11] He also presided over the marriage of Richard Bogle and America Waldo in January 1863; the wedding was a racially mixed social event, a rarity for that time and place. Asahel Bush wrote a letter to his patron Matthew Deady that included mention of the event. It contained a long string of comments that were racist toward the black attendees and hostile to the whites. He concluded, "It was negro equality sentiment mixed up with a little snob-aristocracy. The 'first circle' character of the whites, was expected to give *eclat* to the affair, and bar all remarks. But it has caused a great deal of gossip, and generally [is] regarded as shameful by the community."[12]

Other Oregon clergymen lost their congregations' support in the face of widespread pro-Southern, antiblack sentiment. Rev. Milton Starr left Corvallis in 1862 after his income dried up: "He said ... that the Secession sympathies of many of his people at Corvallis and some also at Albany would render his preaching useless for this summer."[13]

As the war progressed, attitudes did not improve in Salem. In fact, the congregation responded to isolation from the community by gradually reducing support for its minister: he found it increasingly difficult to make a living from parish contributions, and construction on the new church building slowed down. The church's leading parishioners could not reconcile their vision of their church's message with their minister's application of Christian values to African Americans. In a series of resolutions they delivered to Dickinson in early 1863, they stated that while they believed slavery to be "a great evil," they did not want it or any issues of race spoken of from the pulpit, asking him to "abstain from these exciting topics, slavery, etc."[14] Dickinson replied by reiterating his stand.

> In the contest of party for power I have taken no part in the pulpit. If this is what you mean by preaching "politics" I object to the use of the term. ... If on the other hand you mean by politics those great moral principles of justice, righteousness, temperance, and the fear of God, without which the prosperity, peace and safety of the people can never long continue, then in that sense I have preached politics, and by the blessing of God, I hope long to preach it.[15]

The next month, his congregation did not renew his yearlong appointment. As 1863 went on, they completed the church building. However, they also needed American Home Missionary Society financial support for paying a minister, and clergymen were hard to come by, so they rehired Dickinson. He held on to his beliefs, but church support waned again. And the combination of the desire to keep Oregon in the Union and widespread hostility to blacks remained after the war. Dickinson left his church in 1867 after years of financial and political struggle, replaced by a less controversial pastor. He started a prosperous nursery and seed business, setting up shop at 292 Commercial Street, and stayed in Salem until his death in 1892.

❖

In 2010, Dinah, Jan, and Pam Kinney, Obed Dickinson's great-great-great-granddaughters, donated a precious family heirloom—a blue and white coverlet that had once belonged to Dickinson and his wife—to the Oregon Northwest Black Pioneers for inclusion in the future Oregon African American Museum collection. It was originally created for Dickinson's father in 1820 and was among the household items the Dickinsons brought with them on their journey around Cape Horn to Oregon.

Dinah Kinney says about donating the coverlet, "It's not ours anymore. It belongs to the history of Oregon."[16]

6

Later Nineteenth-Century Profiles

"Father Bayless, Born a Slave in Tennessee, Has Lived to an Honorable old Age Under the Free Skies of Oregon"

As the nineteenth century progressed, African Americans continued to arrive in the Salem area, making homes for themselves and contributing to their communities. Here are profiles of a few of them.

Albert and Mary Bayless

Born into slavery in Tennessee on August 15, 1819, Albert Bayless (sometimes spelled Bales) reportedly spent his first thirty years working for a "kind master." When this man died, Albert was sold to a much crueler man. Somehow, Albert managed to escape to California "during the great mining excitement." It is unknown exactly when he made his way to Salem, but once there, he set up a blacksmith shop. Eventually he became known locally as "Father Bayless."

Bayless was active in the Methodist church, one of only two churches that allowed African Americans to attend at that time.

Book of Remembrance offers a description of both the character and appearance of Bayless and his wife, Mary.

The only other neighbor I recollect was Mr. Bayless, the colored blacksmith, who worked at the shop just beside us on the corner. He was such a kindly old man, with his kinky locks, fast turning gray, and somewhere hidden about that old shop were sticks of red striped candy to give to the children who stopped to talk with him on their way from school. This little old colored man, with his good wife, so many shades darker than he and of ponderous build, will be remembered by all early Salem folk for their good deeds and Christian lives. In their hospitable home a white boy was raised to manhood. On Sunday morning they were welcomed to their particular corner, up near the pulpit and at the southwest side of the auditorium of the first M.E. church, of which they were acceptable members.

Albert lived an exceptionally long life, dying on April 18, 1907, at the age of eighty-eight. For the last ten years of his life, he was blind and nearly helpless.[1]

The September 23, 1906, *Daily Oregon Statesman* carried an article about Albert's eighty-seventh birthday party, summarized "Father Bayless, Born a Slave in Tennessee, Has Lived to an Honorable old Age Under the Free Skies of Oregon—Is Devoted Methodist—Eigh-Seventh [sic] Birthday Celebrated." The article relates how Albert found his future wife: "One day he walked westward to view Polk county, but came away satisfied with the sight of one of Polk county's women, who has been to him a faithful companion these many years." The article goes on to offer a flavor of the birthday event.

These annual celebrations are of more than local interest, as on that day friends fill the house to assist in the observance of the passing of another milestone in life's long journey. The contributions of money and groceries made this worthy couple to praise the bounty of their faithful friends and the goodness of

The headstone of Albert and Mary Ann Bayless in the Salem Pioneer Cemetery, placed in May 2002

their Heavenly Father whose care they believe with the confidence of little children. Their faith and hope and freedom from petulancy or complaining brings blessings to all who enter their humble home.

Mary Ann Bayless was born a slave in Bowling Green, Kentucky, around 1823. In Mary we have a slavery story uncommon among the pre–Civil War African American arrivals to Oregon; at age sixteen she had been granted freedom. She then moved to Missouri and married a man named David Reynolds, and the couple had four children. Her husband and two daughters died, and in 1864 she moved to Oregon with her two remaining children, traveling with the James Ord family. She, too, lived an unusually long time, but outlived

Albert by less than a week, dying April 24, 1907, at the age of eighty-four. She had been ill for some months before her death, but the cause of death was attributed to grief over losing her longtime companion.

Hiram Gorman

Hiram Gorman (sometimes spelled Gorham) was born in Missouri around 1835 and was likely one of several slaves owned by Thomas Gorman of Macon, Missouri. We do not know how he made his way to Oregon, but we do know that he served with the Union forces as a teamster during the Civil War, and that after spending time in Montana beginning in 1864, he arrived here in 1871.

Hiram was the son of Hannah Gorman, who came to Oregon in 1844 with her daughter and Hiram's sister, Eliza. At that time, Hannah and Eliza bore the last name of Thorp, their owner at the time. Both would return to the Gorman name later on. While Hiram evidently hadn't seen his mother or sister for more than a quarter century, a few years after coming to Oregon he would be involved in a real estate transaction concerning property they owned in Corvallis, and it is thought that Hannah lived with him and his family shortly before her death (see Hannah and Eliza's story in chapter 2).

Hiram lived in Salem at the corner of Liberty and Chemeketa streets. He was well liked in the community and known for his gardening skills. A June 14, 1871, article in the *Oregon Statesman* noted that he had brought to the newspaper office a pea stalk "grown on his plantation" measuring seven feet three inches long. A July 23, 1879, *Statesman* article had more to say about Gorman's green thumb, noting that he had "one of the finest gardens we have noticed in the city" and that he had brought the newspaper a "nice bunch of beans, which for

Hiram Gorman's headstone in the Pioneer Cemetery, placed in May 2002

size, at this season of the year, are hard to surpass."

There is a good reason the newspaper was so well acquainted with Gorman as to be treated to his produce: he worked for a number of years as the newspaper's pressman, beginning shortly after he arrived in town and ending only when his job was automated by steam motor in 1883: "... for 12 years a giant negro, Hiram Gorman, was the *Statesman's* 'engine.'"[2]

Gorman's wife's name was Georgia Ann, and the couple had three children: Emma, William, and Frank. *The Book of Remembrance* offers an anecdote about Gorman's ten-year-old son (referred to as "Bud," likely Frank) in a chapter called "A Memorable Winter in a Little Girl's Life," the winter of 1880–81. Frank, "a smart little rascal and sort of cute looking" would tease the girl by waiting for her to head to school and then falling in step beside her "as if we were pals." "This embarrassed me so," she says, "for being very bashful and also realizing I had the family traditions to uphold, I really got to hate that fun-loving colored lad. I would walk blocks out of my way to avoid him and I would not have looked at him for the world."

Hiram died on July 23, 1888, just three weeks after the death of his mother. The affection the community accorded him was evident in his obituary in the *Statesman*.

> "Hi" was a well-known character in Salem, and was universally liked for his unfailing good nature and for his large-hearted generosity. His acts of kindness were innumerable. For some months preceding his death, he was an invalid, and unable to do any work, but he was sustained at home by relatives and friends.

Georgia Ann Gorman passed away a little more than three years after her husband, on October 10, 1891.

John W. Jackson: From Union Soldier to "Well-to-Do Colored Man"

John W. Jackson was born in 1839. We don't know why or when he came to Oregon, but we do know that before he traveled west he "was one among 180,000 African American soldiers who fought for the Union." Records show that he served with the 5th Cavalry U.S. Colored Troops.[3] He apparently enlisted as a sergeant and was promoted to sergeant major in 1863.[4]

Here in Oregon, John W. Jackson lived near Hayesville in Marion County and was a member of the Hayesville Farmers Club, a grange-style organization. According to the 1952 research notes of deceased local historian George Strozut Jr., based on church clerks' record books, old scrapbooks, personal interviews, research in the state archives, and early newspapers, the club was organized in 1886 and was said to be the first of its kind in the state. In its minutes we find references to Jackson taking part in discussions at their meetings:

> What causes more rust on wheat in a wet season than in a dry one? Answered by Mr. Jackson. He thought it was caused by small insects.

Evidently, Jackson's wife, Carolyn, participated in Club meetings as well:

> Mrs. Jackson gave the geological classification and origin of the stones usually found in the beds of streams. This closed the question drawer.

An article from the time about the Farmers Club, likely published in the *Woodburn Independent*, indicates its leadership and its egalitarian nature:

> The Hayesville Farmers Club has been organized about two years, with A. Stephens of Salem Grange as President, and J. W. Jackson (a colored man) as Secretary. Our object is education on all subjects that interest the farmer. We have our constitution and By-laws. Any person, old or young, male or female, may become a member, who will attend and participate in

The markers of John W. Jackson (above and opposite page) and wife Caroline (opposite page) at Hayesville Cemetery

the exercises. Any person is eligible to office, without regard to sex.

"A. Stephens" was Adam Stephens, who wrote poetry under the pen name "A Bystander." In one poem he refers to his "neighbor, J. Jackson, a negro." Stephens also chronicled community activities in the *Independent* under this pen name. (See p. 98 for a photo of his gravestone.)

John W. Jackson died February 25, 1892, and is buried in

the Hayesville Cemetery. According to the February 26, 1892, *Oregon Statesman* obituary, he died at his home from pneumonia. The piece describes Jackson this way:

> Deceased was a well-to-do colored man who has made his home in the vicinity of Hayesville for several years. He was road supervisor for several terms.

Caroline Jackson, born in Jackson County, Iowa, lived to be eighty-nine years old, at last succumbing to the same

Adam Stephens's gravestone at Hayesville Cemetery

illness that befell her husband forty-one years earlier. According to the *Oregon Statesman*, January 7, 1933, she left "one son, George C. Jackson of Salem."

The most recent mention we find about John W. Jackson comes from an unidentified source that may be a church record book. It lists the following facts of Adam Stephens's life:

Kept bees
Played croquet
Taught singing
Played organ with special keys
…
Adam stopped train

" 	had blacksmith shop
" 	never owned overalls
" 	made own suits out of black broadcloth ...
...
Family kept slaves
Neighbor was J. Jackson, negro
" 		buried near him

Annie Smith, Johnny Jones, and Amanda Titus

The 1910 federal census lists Anna ("Annie") E. Smith as fifty-seven years old, widowed, and the head of her household. Living with her at this time in a small house near Market and Fifth in Salem were her brother, John ("Johnny") M. Jones, fifty-two, and their mother, Amanda Titus, seventy. All are described as mulattos. (Later censuses categorize Annie as black or Negro.) From a Marion County census the same year, we learn that both Anna and John were born in California. Amanda was born in Tennessee.

Malinda Johnson, now in her eighties, still remembers "Auntie Smith" as a fixture at Salvation Army church services she attended as a child. She was a kind, heavyset woman who used to sit in a big oak chair beside the pot-bellied woodstove in the corner of the building, often with a child on her lap: members of the congregation would bring her their sleepy or fidgety children because she had a knack for calming them. Malinda was one of those children, and she still has fond memories of Auntie's smile and her comfortable lap.

Johnson's description of Smith as "heavyset" is corroborated in an 1895 "Enumeration of Inhabitants and Industrial Products," which, interestingly, includes figures for height and weight. Annie Smith is just five feet tall and weighs 186 pounds. Her occupation is listed as "laundress." Incidentally,

Though it is no longer the Salvation Army facility where Annie Smith tended to the congregation's children, this building on State Street near Commercial still bears traces of the old sign.

brother Johnny did not share his sister's body type—he was five-eight and 140 pounds.[5]

What is most remarkable about Annie Smith is the position she held within the Salvation Army. She joined the organization in 1895. In 1911, a time when Salem's African Americans did not worship with whites, let alone hold respected positions within a church organization, she attained

The gravestone of Annie Smith and Johnny Jones and their mother, Amanda Titus, at City View Cemetery, placed by Oregon Northwest Black Pioneers and the Salvation Army in 2011

the rank of ward sergeant. She was put in charge of selling the Army's magazine, *Warcry*, and she assisted the field officer in his pastoral duties, visiting church members in their homes. She sat with the sick, prayed with family members, and looked after the needs of women in the congregation (a male ward sergeant worked with the men). In 2007, the curator of the Salvation Army Museum of the West commented: "It is of course remarkable that a black woman in Oregon at the turn of the century was asked to help look after the spiritual needs of the congregation."

Annie died on May 16, 1937, in Portland. In 1938 she was removed from Salvation Army rolls. The stated reason for the removal: she had been "promoted to glory."

Johnny's story is noteworthy as well. An August 25, 1932, *Oregon Statesman* article upon his death describes him as a "genial colored man and long-time resident"; he was known to have lived in Salem at least since the 1880s. The article tells us Johnny held a job (unspecified) at the Chemeketa hotel and worked for at least two restaurants in town, but he apparently was best known for his catering business: "He was always in demand as a caterer at private homes, and the phrase 'Johnny Jones feed' was always sure to bring a capacity crowd to a lodge dinner."

Two days after this article was published, the paper ran a piece announcing upcoming funeral services for Johnny. In it, he is described as a "caterer to many local social and lodge functions." The community respect he enjoyed is evident from those who chose to be his pallbearers: members of the Elks lodge and "a number of prominent Salem area residents."

Amanda Titus, a former slave, was both a housekeeper and a nurse. She died June 7, 1916, at the estimated age of eighty.

All three members of the family are buried at Salem's City View Cemetery. A stone has recently been placed in their honor, a joint project of the Salvation Army and the Oregon Northwest Black Pioneers.

Louis Southworth

On June 27, 2010, a community fiddle jam was held at Crystal Lake Cemetery in Corvallis, Oregon. The event was a celebration in honor of a well-known African American Oregonian who is buried at the cemetery: Louis Alexander Southworth.

Southworth was born into slavery in Tennessee in 1830. He came to Oregon with his master, James Southworth, in 1851, settling in Marysville (later Corvallis).

In 1856 Louis went to the gold country in southern Oregon near Jacksonville, aiming to raise $1,000 to buy his freedom. He earned a down payment of $300 during the trip. On his way back from Jacksonville, he was essentially drafted into fighting in the Rogue River Indian War when confronted by soldiers who threatened to take his rifle from him. Rather than travel home without protection, he joined Colonel John Kelsay's Second Regiment. He fought in two battles and suffered wounds in one of them.

In 1858 he traveled to Yreka, California, to work as a musician, having discovered that he could make more money by entertaining people with his fiddle than by mining gold. There he earned another $400 to pay his master.

The following year, Louis made his last payment and obtained his freedom, although this was never formalized on paper. After freeing Louis, James Southworth circulated a petition in Lane County to protect "slave property," which went to the state legislature.

In 1870, Louis Southworth settled in Buena Vista in Polk County and ran a blacksmith shop and livery stable. Three years later he married Mary Cooper in Salem. The new family (she had an adopted son, Alvin) lived in Buena Vista for a few years, where Alvin attended the Buena Vista Academy and the school's principal taught Louis to read.

The Southworths moved to Alsea Bay in 1880 along with Jim Doty, a white friend. They decided to homestead about four miles north of Waldport, and Louis ferried cargo and people up and down the Alsea River for years. Louis once joked, "Jim Doty and I were the first two white men on the Alsea Bay."

Mary died in 1901. In 1910, Louis moved to Corvallis, where he bought a house at the corner of Fourth and Adams. He died in 1917.[6]

Throughout his life in Oregon, Southworth was active in his community. At Alsea Bay, for example, he donated land for a school and became chairman of the school board.[7]

In February 2005 he was honored in the *Congressional*

Record as "one of Oregon's most respected and well-liked citizens of his time."[8]

Southworth made his lifelong love of music clear in a 1915 interview with the *Daily Gazette-Times*. His fellow parishioners at the Baptist church in Waldport had barred him from attending because of his fiddle playing.

> But the brethren would not stand for my fiddle, which was about all the company I had much of the time. So, I told them to keep me in the church with my fiddle, if they could, but to turn me out if they must, for I could not think of parting with the fiddle. I reckon my name wasn't written in their books here anymore, but I somehow hope it's written in the big book up yonder where they aren't so particular about fiddles.[9]

These are the people from this era about whom we have the most information, but we know of others, thanks to the Salem Pioneer Cemetery, the subject of the next chapter.

Salem in 1876: a bird's-eye view from the west

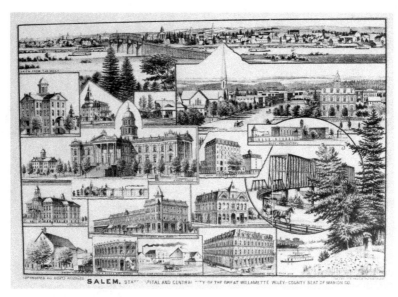

Salem's major buildings, 1888

7

At Rest
in the
Salem Pioneer
Cemetery

The 2007 dedication ceremony for a headstone listing the names of all African Americans known to be buried at the Salem Pioneer Cemetery, presented by the Oregon Northwest Black Pioneers

Two people whom you met in chapter 2 are buried in the Salem Pioneer Cemetery, located at the intersection of South Commercial and Hoyt streets in Salem: Jackson Bonter, along with members of his family, and Robin Holmes. Albert and Mary Bayless and Hiram Gorman from chapter 5 are also here. Several other African Americans are buried here as well, and they are the subject of this chapter.

It is worth noting that blacks and whites were not segregated in this cemetery as they often were elsewhere.

As you will see, scant information is available about most of the individuals we profile here. Some of them might have been more properly included in the earlier chapter on wagon train arrivals (George Washington is one example, having come to the area in the early 1850s), but because we were unable to know with certainty that they traveled here that way, we have grouped them in this chapter instead.

We are grateful to the Friends of Pioneer Cemetery for their careful recording of dates of birth and death, obituary text, and other surviving snippets of information. Because these sources are already well documented on the cemetery's web site (www. salempioneercemetery.org), we do not always include sources for this chapter in the Notes section at the back of the book. We encourage you to visit the web site, which has a user-friendly search function. For a more personal experience and direct connection to the Salem area's African American past, we also invite you to explore the cemetery itself. Where lot numbers are available, we have listed them.

Beulah Alexander
Beulah Alexander was born in Alabama in 1886 and died on June 17, 1921. The occupation listed at the time of her death was housewife. Although she had been living in Portland, she died at a local hospital.

Martha Barker
Martha Barker was born in Mississippi in 1843. Her 1915 obituary reads in part:

> FAITHFUL COLORED SERVANT DIES
> "Mammy," the aged colored servant whom the D. I. Howard family brought from the south a year ago, died yesterday at a local hospital after twenty years of faithful service in a family where she was much respected. Her unexpected death has brought a shock of grief to her employers. (*Oregon Statesman,* June 6, 1915, 5:4, 5)
> (Lot 912)

John Barrand
Barrand was born in Harrisburg, Pennsylvania, in 1894. At the time of his death at Salem Hospital in 1914, his occupation was laborer. (Lot 705)

Ernest Beste
Born in Cuba in 1870, Beste immigrated to the United States in 1903. He died in 1911 of tuberculosis. From his obituary: "Earnest Befte, aged 31 years. He leaves a wife but no children, and had been a porter at the Gilson barber shop." (*Daily Oregon Statesman*, March 9, 1911.) A census listed his occupation as "wagon expressman." (Lot 356)

Mary "Mazie" Elizabeth Brooks
Known as "Auntie" Brooks according to her obituary, Mary Elizabeth Brooks was born about 1860 and died in 1947:

> Mrs. Mazie (Auntie) Brooks, 87, well known Salem woman, died at her home, 1318 N. Commercial Street, late last night. ... There are no known survivors ... Born in Pennsylvania, Mrs. Brooks had traveled throughout the United States and spent one year in Alaska. She spent a year in the east after the death of her husband in 1926. A member of the Independent Order of Good Temperance, "Auntie" Brooks held, at different times all the offices of the organization. An active worker in the first world war, she was not able to participate in war work during world war II. Annually she placed flowers on the world war monument in the courthouse square. (*Oregon Statesman*, March 7, 1947.)
> (Lot 365)

William Brown
Brown was born in Missouri in 1872. His wife's name was Zella. A bootblack by trade, Brown died in 1924.

The grave marker of Stanley Charmon

Stanley Charmon
Born in Minneapolis in 1903, Charmon was a logger. He died in the Oregon State Penitentiary in 1937. A headstone marks his grave. (Lot FA 03)

Alfred Drake
Drake was born in Kentucky in 1822 and died in 1875. He was a laborer. (Lot 369)

Elizabeth Drake
Alfred's wife was born in Missouri in 1837. Her obituary reads in part: "Mrs. Drake, a colored woman, who resided above Independence, died last Tuesday. She leaves a husband and 5 children." (*The Daily Oregon Unionist,* September 2, 1869.) (Lot 369)

Elizabeth L. Drake

Alfred and Elizabeth's daughter was born in 1868. She did not live long: "... a babe, 16 months old, daughter of Mrs. Drake, (colored) of Independence, who died last fall." (*Weekly Oregon Statesman*, March 11, 1870.) (Lot 369)

Joseph (Joe) Drake

Joe Drake, son of Alfred and Elizabeth, was born about 1856 in Missouri. He was a farm laborer. Joe was hanged in 1885 for a murder he swore he had not committed. Many others in the community believed him; "Numerous jurists and the majority of public opinion felt the young black man had been falsely convicted." Still, no one was willing to come to his defense, and he was hanged in a public spectacle at the Marion County Courthouse on March 20, 1885. In a statement to the assembled crowd he said:

> I have not much to say. I am going to be executed for a crime I know nothing about. I am about to die for a deed committed by other hands. It looks hard. ... I think it is pretty hard that I have to lay down my life like this. I can't say who did the work, for I was not there. I know I have been rudely dealt with. I thank the people who have tried to help me for their kindness ... I am going to die for the company I have kept, not for any crime I have committed. This should be a warning to every boy and everybody else. I have run with all sorts of company, and I am here for it. I have harmed no one. It was my company. I don't hold any hard feelings for my persecutors. Maybe they thought they were doing right.

An article in the *Weekly Oregon Statesman* dated March 27, 1885, described the funeral.

> The funeral of Joseph Drake, who was executed last Friday, took place on Sunday. The colored people of the city were all in attendance and a number of carriages containing white ladies and gentlemen were in the procession. Religious services were held at the grave and the last act of the tragedy closed decently, leaving only the record of its ghastly debate on the memory of those conversant with the fact and circumstances by which is was surrounded.
> (Lot 202)

Charles Fralix
Fralix lived from about 1882 to May 17, 1917. A porter for the Southern Pacific, he died, aged about thirty-five, aboard a train between Woodburn and Salem. (Lot 598)

Ohmar Parker Grigsby
Grigsby was born December 30, 1884, and died April 1, 1914. His occupation was listed as bootblack. His usual residence had been Portland. (Lot 750)

Sybil Haber
Cemetery records say Sybil Haber was born in Missouri in December 1856 (although the 1910 census lists her as fifty-six years old, putting her year of birth at 1853 or 1854). She moved to Lakeview, Oregon, in 1888 and was a well-respected nurse and midwife. She died on Armistice Day, November 11, 1918. (Some biographical material spells her name Harber.) (Lot 773)

OrHi 07000

Sybil Haber

Wilbert D. Henderson

Henderson was born in 1888 and was a porter in a barber shop. He died July 25, 1937, age forty-six, of drowning near Foster. (Lot FA 47)

Wilbert Henderson's gravestone

J. C. Jackson

Jackson, a cook, was born about 1835 and died April 22, 1900. He was memorialized in the April 24, 1900, *Oregon Statesman:*

> At his home in this city, corner of Mill and Broadway streets, North Salem. ... The deceased was the well-known colored man of North Salem. Though not a native of Oregon, Mr. Jackson was for many years a resident of this state. He lived in Salem for about ten years, during a part of which he was employed as cook at the Indian Training school at Chemawa and the State Reform School.
>
> He went to Baker City last fall where he worked for several months as a cook. In February he was taken sick and after spending five weeks in the Baker City hospital was sent back to his family in this city, reaching Salem about four weeks ago. Salem physicians were unable to satisfactorily diagnose his case and

The gravestone of J. C. Jackson

no one was able to ascertain the true nature of his ailment.

Besides a son and daughter, residing in Portland, the deceased is survived by a wife and three children, the latter aged, two, four and nine years, in this city. (Lot 370)

Rosetta Bonter Johnson
Rosetta was born the daughter of Jackson and Mary Bonter. William and Elizabeth Johnson adopted her after her mother, Mary, died. She was born January 8, 1879, and died aged ten on December 28, 1889. (See p. 33 for a photo of her gravestone.)

Samuel Johnson
A barber, Johnson was born in Connecticut in 1827. From the *Oregon Statesman* obituary:

DEATH WITHOUT WARNING—A Colored Barber Found Dead—Coroner's Inquest—Verdict, Heart Disease. About 4 o'clock Sunday, June 22d, 1873, Samuel Johnson, a colored barber of this city was found lying dead in the rear of his barber shop on Commercial Street. ... He had no relatives in Oregon and left no means to defray the expense of his burial, and Mr. Coffee [the coroner], therefore caused the body to be decently buried at the expense of the county. ... Johnson had been drinking some the preceding night and during Sunday; and when found, it was first supposed that he was merely drunk. ... He had been during the day sky-larking with a German known as "Dutch Jo" or "Lager Beer Jo," and once or twice he had threatened to whip Jo and had struck him, appearing to be greatly excited. These circumstances led to the arrest of Jo, but upon hearing the evidence before the Coroner's Jury, he was at once discharged.
(Lot 363)

Charles Earnest Letcher

Letcher was born in St. Charles, Missouri, on December 28, 1878. He died May 2, 1946. His cemetery record offers two widely varying accounts: a personal recollection by one John Davis says Letcher was born in Missouri and "brought to Oregon when he was a very small boy by a Southern gentleman who owned him as a slave" (although he was apparently born after Emancipation) and lived with his "master" in Corvallis until the man died. According to his obituary, however, Letcher was born on a plantation in Georgia, was brought to

Oregon by the plantation owner family, the Bests, and lived in the Four Corners area of east Salem. (Lot FA 48)

Roxanna Miller

Roxanna was born about 1847 to Robin and Polly Holmes and died July 22, 1873, of "consumption " (tuberculosis). See chapter 3 for more detail on the Holmes family. (Lot 202)

Marion Parks

Marion Parks was born September 13, 1850, and died December 5, 1868. Mary, his twin sister, married Jackson Bonter; see chapter 2 for more information about the Bonter family. (Lot 191)

Maggie Adeline Randles

Randles was born ca. 1852 and died of pneumonia on April 30, 1907. There was a notice of her wedding in the *Oregon Statesman*, July 22, 1894:

> MARRIED: At the residence of A. Bayless, in North Salem, at 2 p.m., Saturday, July 21, 1894, George Randles and Miss M.A. Stanley, Rev. J Bowersox officiating.
>
> The newly wedded couple are colored residents of Marion county and their home in the future will be on a farm north of Salem. The groom is well known in Salem having been a driver for a Salem transfer company for many years and a member of the old volunteer fire department.

Her obituary in the May 2, 1907, *Daily Oregon Statesman* reads:

Sister and brother: the gravestone of Mary Parks
Bonter and Marion Parks

RANDLES—At the Salem hospital, April 30, 1907, Mrs.
Maggie Adeline Randles, aged 55 years, of pneumonia. Mrs. Randles is survived by her husband, George
Randles, of this city. … Mrs. Randles for a long time
past had cared for Mr. And Mrs. Albert Bayliss, the
aged colored couple who died recently in North Salem. She has been a resident of Salem for many years
and leaves many friends here.
(Lot 369)

Frank W. Smith

Frank Smith was an Adventist preacher, born in Texas on April 16, 1861. He died December 10, 1931. (Lot 759)

Gus Trollinger

Trollinger was born May 17, 1890, in Huntsville, Missouri. His cemetery record lists him as a longshoreman and a railroad laborer. He died September 3, 1941, leaving his wife and two children. (Lot 778)

George Washington

Washington was born a slave in Virginia about 1816 and died June 5, 1891. His obituary in the June 7 *Daily Oregon Statesman* reads:

> "Uncle George" Washington, the old colored man who has been known to residents of Salem for so many years, is dead. He passed to his reward yesterday morning and his death will be generally regretted. Uncle George was about 75 years old and came to Salem early in the 50's as a slave. He worked for many years as a servant about the hotel and was formerly the property of Calvin Hanna. He also was in the service of Governor Gibbs for a number of years.
>
> He came here from Roseburg under contract to "Brad" Robinson. The death of this faithful old Virginian removes a familiar face from the streets of Salem where this old darkey had lived happily through adversity and prosperity, through slavery and freedom. He died of old age. The funeral will be conducted at 2 p.m. today from the residence of Mrs. Titus.
> (Lot 260)

George T. Williams

Born in California about 1864, Williams was a schoolboy when he died of drowning in the Willamette River at West Salem on May 6, 1873.

> DROWNED—A small boy, son of George Williams, colored, was drowned in the Willamette river opposite Salem, about 5 o'clock last evening. *(Oregon Statesman,* May 7,1873)

> BODY FOUND—The steamer *Fannie Patton* arrived yesterday morning from down the river bringing the intelligence that the body of George Williams, the colored boy drowned in the Willamette opposite Salem, some weeks ago, had been found in a pile of drift at or near Lincoln, a few miles below here. The boy's father immediately procured a coffin and started upon the melancholy errand of recovering and bringing home his dead boy. *(Oregon Statesman,* June 21, 1873)
> (Lot 365)

James F. Williams

James was born August 2, 1873, and died an infant on September 2 of "inflammation of the brain." (Lot 365)

Jesse Williams

Williams was born in Rappahannock, Virginia, May 18, 1801. He married Nancy Bonter on July 17, 1860. His occupations were listed as mason (1860 census) and gardener (1870). He died of colic in Salem on October 21, 1871. His obituary reads:

Jesse Williams's grave

Died—In this vicinity on Friday, Jesse Williams, an aged colored man. The funeral services of Uncle Jesse Williams, will be held this morning at eleven o'clock at the colored school house. The Rev. Daniel Jones will conduct the exercises. *(Oregon Statesman,* October 22, 1871)
(Lot 361)

Nancy Williams
Jesse's wife, Nancy Bonter Williams, was born in Kentucky about 1803. She died in September 1882 in Portland of "old age." For more information on the Bonter family, see chapter 2. (Lot 365)

Salem Pioneer Cemetery

On this page and the next, the layout of the Salem Pioneer Cemetery. The entrance is off Hoyt Street, east of City View Cemetery.

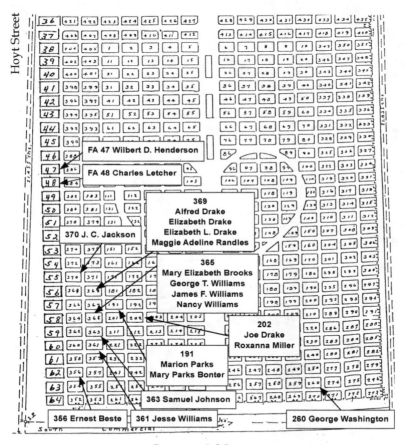

Commercial Street

125

8

Into the Twentieth Century: 1900 through *Brown vs. Board*

Two Views of Salem at the Turn of the Century

The old Marion County Courthouse, built in 1873 and razed in 1952 (photographed in 1903). The old state capitol is in the background.

A postcard showing Wallace Road in West Salem, 1912. The message on the back includes "…after you leave the old Harritt place going towards town… That flat strip between Harritts and the negro woman's place…" The "old Harritt place" is now Julia's Tea Parlor.

The Civil War and Reconstruction came and went, leaving little in the way of progress toward equality in America or in Oregon. According to the 1900 federal census, the state's black population stood at 1,105: 0.2 percent of the overall total. And closer to home, according to an NAACP report in 1936, "Salem has no Negro population, except a few inmates in the Penal Institution and Insane Hospital." White Oregonians continued their opposition to the African American presence, and this could be seen statewide.

In 1905, black Portlander Oliver Taylor sued the management of the Star Theater for refusing him admission to a box seat. The judge found for the theater on the grounds that it could refuse anyone, regardless of race. The *Oregonian* was more transparent in its editorial supporting the decision:

> If one person—a Chinaman, for example—has a right to buy any seat in the house, and sit in it, may any other person—a Hottentot, or a woman of notorious reputation—do the same thing? It is not a question as to whether a white person objects to sitting next to a Chinaman. It is simply a well-known fact that he does object, and the theater must govern itself accordingly.[1]

A parade on Court Street, early twentieth century. Behind the
Grand Opera House (right) is the Marion County Courthouse.

McCants Stewart, the first black person admitted to the
Oregon bar, fought successfully for Taylor, winning a judg-
ment for him in the state supreme court.[2] The Portland city
government came close to outlawing racial association in the
1920s. A black nightclub owner saw his cabaret license revoked in 1922 when police raided the place and found white
women dancing with black men. He appealed the revocation
but the city council upheld it unanimously. It also considered an ordinance banning interracial dancing. The mayor
said that while no law forbade racial association, the law of
common decency did.[3] Oregon restaurants, whether they
displayed "Whites only" signs or not, discriminated against
blacks. And while the local NAACP campaigned to persuade

A "We cater to white trade only" sign in Portland

OrHi ba018361

restaurant owners to take the signs down, removal was voluntary until the passage of the 1953 public accommodations law.[4] African Americans also faced difficulty in finding housing. For example, as long as there were few black people in Portland, they could live wherever they could afford to. But as their numbers increased, racist real estate practices took hold. Starting in 1919, the Portland Realty Board added a provision to its code of ethics: members were forbidden to sell housing in white neighborhoods to blacks or Asians. Even after World War II, the board expelled a realtor for selling property in a white area to a black person.[5]

The Advocate, a leading African American newspaper in Portland, summarized the evil effects of segregation:

It means poor housing, bad streets, and if the streets are paved, poorly kept, deficient lighting. It also means separate schools and their attendant shortcomings. It invites race riots because ... any attempt on the part of

OrHi bb06959

A Highway Department crew spread "hot stuff" on the Pacific Highway, one of the main trunks in the state plan, near Jefferson in the mid-twentieth century.

the weaker [race] to exercise its rights of liberty, at all, is met with opposition from the stronger; the trouble begins. It is segregation that is the root of all interracial troubles.[6]

Smaller communities were at least equally hostile. A front-page editorial in Grants Pass's *Southern Oregon Spectator,* May 24, 1924, asserted that "Grants Pass has always been a white man's town and there is no reason under the shining sun why it shouldn't continue to be a white man's town." It had this message, in all capital letters, for "the black, brown or red faces of the land": NIGGER WE DON'T WANT YOU HERE—WE WON'T HAVE YOU HERE—YOU HAD BETTER ROLL UP YOUR BED AND RIDE—THIS IS TO BE A WHITE MAN'S COUNTRY, YESTERDAY, TODAY, AND FOREVER.

Klavern 29, the West's Largest

The Oregon Ku Klux Klan boasted of 14,000 members in 1922. Klavern 29 in Salem, with a thousand, was said to be the largest west of the Mississippi.

Salem's postmaster led the local Klan. Members met at theaters downtown, including the Grand, the Elsinore, and the Reed Opera House. They marched in full regalia in local parades, complete with floats. Their march through the streets of Salem in 1923 was said to be the longest parade the city had ever seen.

In addition to threatening and attacking black citizens (see the Charles Maxwell incident, p. 139), Salem Klansmen targeted Chinese, Catholics, Jews, and other minorities. A once thriving Chinese community disappeared from Salem during the 1920s under Klan pressure and violence.

Late one night in 1921, hooded Klansmen planted a cross at Salem's Sacred Heart Convent and were about to light it when the Mother Superior came out and aimed her shotgun at them, greeting them with "Good evening gentlemen. I will count to four, and send you all to perdition. One, two—" The men said, "Aw, sister, we were just fooling around!" They picked up the tarred cross and threw it into the bed of their pickup truck. She commanded, "Wait! Fill in the hole and smooth the ground, Mr. Mayor. You help, Mr. Sheriff. Now!" Despite their hoods, she recognized the mayor by his dog in the truck and identified the sheriff by his distinctive boots, made by a Jewish cobbler on Liberty Street.

Thanks to local historian John Ritter for this information, based on his presentation at the Salem Public Library.

Closer to home, a 1927 promotional piece for Salem ("Trail 'em to Salem"), after praising its scenery and landmarks, boasted that it was "The most All-American city in the United States. No foreign element, no Mexicans, 30 negroes and there hasn't been an Indian living in the city for 35 years." Salem's population at that time was 26,500. Twenty years later, Salem was 99 percent white and "91% native born."[7]

During the 1920s, the Ku Klux Klan made its presence felt throughout Oregon, marching in the cities and terrorizing citizens. It wielded enough power to end the political career of Ben Olcott, the Republican governor, who publicly denounced it; the Democratic candidate, Walter Pierce, accepted a Klan endorsement and beat Olcott by a wide margin.[8] "So strong had the Klan become that in Oregon it was able to elect the President of the State Senate and the Speaker of the House."[9]

Klansmen threatened, attacked, and even murdered black men in cities large and small. Two black men were killed in 1924 in Marshfield (later called Coos Bay), a KKK stronghold.[10] In Medford, Klansmen threatened George Burr with hanging. Henry Johnson of Jacksonville received the same treatment; the men who attacked him were later acquitted or the charges against them were dropped. Klansmen nearly lynched Perry Ellis, the only black resident of Oregon City, in 1923. He identified his assailants to the police but no action was taken. A common feature of these attacks is that they were directed against black businessmen in small towns where African Americans were isolated and the Klan was strong. Black Portlanders organized against the KKK, protecting people who were threatened.[11]

In 2009, the January 19 *Statesman Journal* reported on an eyewitness account to Klan activity in Salem: Bruce Williams, then ninety years old, remembered his father taking him to

An Application for Charter Membership in the Klan

A KKK membership application, written in Atlanta and printed in Portland, is in the collection of the Benton County Historical Society in Philomath. It probably dates from the 1920s. In filling it out, the applicant swears to "His Majesty the Imperial Wizard, Emperor of the Invisible Empire, Knights of the KU KLUX KLAN (Inc.)" that he is a white male Gentile "of temperate habits, sound in mind, and a believer in the tenets of the Christian religion, the maintenance of White Supremacy, the practice of an honorable clannishness and the principles of a 'pure Americanism.'"

A series of question follows, beginning with:

1. Is the motive prompting your inquiry serious?

Two questions farther down are curious, considering the initial declaration that the applicant is a white male gentile.

8. Are you a gentile or jew?

9. Are you of the white or of a colored race?

More predictable questions include:

12. Do you believe in the principles of PURE Americanism?

13. Do you believe in White Supremacy?

20. Do you owe ANY KIND of allegiance to any foreign nation, government, institution, sect, people, ruler or person?

Having successfully completed the application, the prospective Klansman had only to accompany it with a $10.00 "donation."

Marion Park when he was in first grade to watch Klansmen assemble on horseback and ride through the center of town. "He wanted me to see that. He had seen persecution before (as a member of the only Protestant family in a midwest Catholic community), and he wanted me to see it firsthand." Photographs from the period show robed Klansmen and children appearing in parades. In one such photo, a Klan-sponsored float is seen at a July 4 parade in Dallas in the 1920s; a sign on the side reads "We hope to see a Bible in every Public School."

While Portland's black students went through de facto school segregation as a result of the city's segregated housing, some Oregon towns were more overt. In 1903, Marshfield imposed separate "but equal" facilities for three children, hiring another teacher rather than letting black and white students mingle. Five students in Vernonia had to go to Portland for schooling until Beatrice Cannady, Oregon's first black woman lawyer, fought successfully to get them admitted to the town's schools.[12] Maxville, a small town near La Grande, banned black children from attending school in 1926; they got their schooling from a black woman in the town who taught them in her home.[13]

During the Depression, black Oregonians found work harder to get. Whites took jobs they had considered beneath them, such as waiter, elevator operator, or janitor. As the war began, many black men worked for the railroads (as waiters, cooks, porters, redcaps, or laborers) and black women could only find work as domestic servants. Unions refused to take on blacks. Even after the state legislature passed a fair employment practices act in 1949 forbidding employment discrimination, unions resisted integration for decades.[14]

The difficulties in finding work may have contributed to a decline in Salem's black population. An NAACP report in

1936 stated: "Salem has no Negro population, except a few inmates in the Penal Institution and Insane Hospital. All of the colored people who did live here have all moved to L.A. I know of no Negroes living in Salem at the present time."[15]

Kathryn Hall Bogle wrote an impassioned and eloquent article in the *Oregonian* in 1937 on her experiences as a black person in white Oregon. She describes how after graduating from high school, she hit the wall of racism in the job market and education: she and a black friend were denied admission to the two largest business schools in Portland. "We found that no Portland hospital will accept the application of a Negro girl for nurse training; there are no Negroes in the employ of the state of Oregon; Negroes have not one representative in the clerical departments of the city. ... Here in Portland there is one Negro secretary... Here, also, one large store has departed from custom and employed a young Negro in a position with some responsibility, albeit behind the scenes."[16]

Sundown Laws

Oregon has a long history of "sundown laws" designed to control the movement of blacks and create a hostile environment for them. Their scope and enforcement have varied by community, reflecting each town's common understanding of what it would tolerate. They subjected blacks to harassment, arrest, and worse after dark. As a result, from the 1890s to the 1930s, the number of Oregon counties with no black residents increased: one county had no African Americans in 1890, and there were four such counties in 1930.[17]

> The white citizens of Liberty, now a South Salem neighborhood, ordered all blacks out of town in 1893 ... [T]he spirit of Liberty lived on for decades. Cities

throughout Oregon adopted "sundown laws," maintained in fact if not by law. Blacks appeared outdoors after dark only at their peril.[18]

Sundown laws would persist well beyond the Civil Rights movement of the sixties.

E. C. Atkinson

A brief item in the *Oregon Statesman* on September 13, 1911, indicates that blacks in Salem were resisting the widespread discrimination of the time. One such person was E. C. Atkinson:

> E. C. Atkinson yesterday filed a suit in the circuit court against F. L. Waters for $5000 damage which he alleges was done him by the refusal of the doorkeepers of the Grand opera house to let him enter the building after he had purchased tickets. He alleges that the refusal was made because he was a negro, and that the humiliation damaged him to that extent.

The actual complaint, filed in Marion County Circuit Court September 12, survives, and in it we learn that the tickets he bought were for himself, his wife, and his son, and when they arrived for the show the usher refused to let the Atkinson family in "in the presence of a large multitude of fashionable people … to the plaintiff's shame, degradation and humiliation." Atkinson then appealed to a Mr. Waters, who also refused them admission. In his response to the complaint, Waters alleged that he did not refuse the Atkinson's admission but instead offered them different seats and a refund. A jury heard the case and ordered Waters to pay Atkinson the cost of the tickets: $3.

Salem's Grand Opera House; Salem City Hall at right (n.d.)

Charles Maxwell

Texas-born Charles Maxwell owned a shoeshine shop in Salem in the 1920s, and offers a good example of perseverance in the face of open hostility. In 1922 he received a letter containing the following text:

> We have stood you as long as we intend to stand you, and you must unload, if you don't we will come to see you.[19]

The author of the letter, which was later published in the *Capital Journal*, was not so forthright as to sign his name, but he had no hesitation about revealing his affiliation; the letter was signed "K.K.K." over a skull and crossbones. This letter may have been a factor in prompting another Salem family, the Halsells, to move to Portland (see chapter 9).

Mrs Charles H. Maxwell of Salem, Oregon, who has charmed many audiences with her sweet voice as a singer. Mrs. Maxwell is one of the race's remarkable women. Mother of eight children, whom she and her husband are rearing admirably, Mrs. Maxwell still finds time for self-improvement.

A newspaper photo of Charles Maxwell's wife, Marie

We do not know how Maxwell responded to this overt act of intimidation, but we know he did not leave town. In 1928 he opened Fat Boy Barbecue, a restaurant in Salem, and ran the business successfully until a bank foreclosure sent him south to Los Angeles.

Maxwell was still in Salem in 1930. Salem city census records list Charles at forty-seven years old, his wife, Marie, at forty-six, and their five children. (A photograph of Marie is on p. 140.) Under the "Industry" column, the record for Charles reads "Barbeque."

The Future Governor as Chauffeur

Early in the 1940s, a famous singer and actor came to Salem, Oregon, to perform for a concert series sponsored by the Columbia Broadcasting System. This tall, strikingly handsome man had by then gained worldwide recognition, having sung at Carnegie Hall and London's Albert Hall, among other renowned venues. He had made a name for himself on stage and in film and radio, and it was remarkable that Salem—then a town of only about thirty-two thousand people—had been able to attract such a talent.

A student at Willamette University who served on the concert series board invited this celebrity to dinner at his fraternity after the concert—a visit that proved a memorable experience for the young man. Afterward, the student drove the singer/actor to Portland for a night's lodging.

The celebrity was the renowned African American singer and actor Paul Robeson.[20]

The student would go on to become state representative, state senator, secretary of state, and then governor of Oregon, and to serve several terms as a United States senator: Mark O. Hatfield.

The trip to Portland had been necessary because, in the early forties, Salem had just two hotels, both owned by the same man, and both of which "saw fit to maintain a straight 'No Coloreds' policy."[21]

This would not be the only time the future governor and senator had to provide such chauffeur service. Sometime later, Marian Anderson, the celebrated contralto, performed for the same concert series. She sang at Salem High School. Salem attorney David Rhoten takes up the story of what followed her recital:

> My mother and other Salem hosts had made reservations for Miss Anderson at the Marion Hotel, Salem's largest and best hotel accommodation. After the concert and a public reception, the hosts brought Miss Anderson to the Marion Hotel to check in at the suite earlier committed for her. ... [U]pon Miss Anderson's entry into the lobby of the hotel and the announcement that she was booked for an accommodation, the night clerk refused to acknowledge the reservation and rejected any and all requests that Miss Anderson be allowed to spend the night. ... The Salem hosts were shocked, embarrassed and chagrined. ...[22]

Once again, Hatfield recounts in his autobiography, "I had to drive our famous performer up to Portland for a night's rest."[23]

Years later, Hatfield would be instrumental in Oregon's passage of a public accommodations law that banned throughout the state the discriminatory policies he had witnessed.

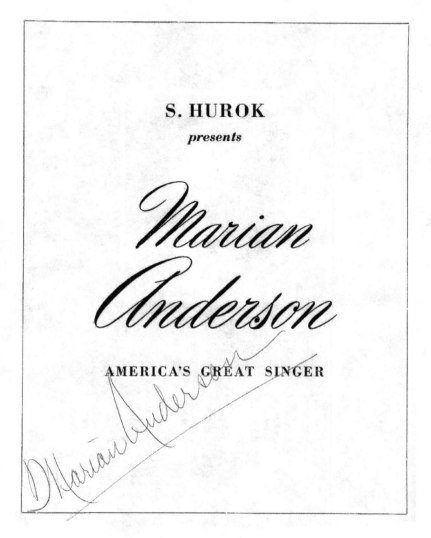

The program from Marian Anderson's Salem concert,
autographed by the singer

The cover of the program for Marian Anderson's Salem concert

Vanport

The community of Vanport reflected the population growth and economic changes that World War II made possible in Oregon; its rise and fall play an important part in the state's black history.

The Housing Authority of Portland (HAP) created this "instant town" between Vancouver, Washington, and Portland (hence the name) in 1943 to house workers for the equally rapidly built Kaiser shipyards on both sides of the Columbia River. It was the largest war housing project in America and at its peak it was also the second biggest city in Oregon: forty thousand residents, 40 percent of whom were black.[24]

While Vanport was more integrated in public accommodations, education, and labor than most other places in Oregon, de facto housing segregation remained in force. White Southern workers objected to the mingling of the races and forced HAP to roll back attempts to integrate the town's housing.[25]

As the war ended, most of Vanport's residents moved away in search of other work; the population dropped to eighteen thousand.

On Memorial Day 1948, a flood inundated Vanport. It killed fifteen people and destroyed the town, which never recovered. (Delta Park and Portland International Raceway were built where it had stood.) But it left a pioneering legacy: Oregon's first black policemen and teachers were hired there during the war.[26] And while Lester Granger, director of the National Urban League, called it a "nasty, segregated ghetto" where "negroes lived in the same patterns as they did in the South," he believed that the flood had a positive effect as black residents moved into north Portland, integrating the city to an unprecedented degree.[27]

While Portland had the highest concentration of African American population in the state, the number was still small. Census figures reflect the demographic change that the war brought about.

1940: Oregon total 1,089,684; black, 2,565 (0.2%)

1940: Portland total 305,394; black, about 2,000 (0.6%)[28]

1950: Oregon total 1,521,341; black, 11,529 (0.7%)[29]

1950: Portland 373,628;[30] black, 9,500 (2.5%)[31]

Salem resident Jackie Winters and her family moved from Topeka, Kansas, to Vanport during World War II. They moved to Portland after the 1948 flood. Jackie went on to become a successful businesswoman in Salem and later state representative and senator from South Salem.

The postwar forties saw Salem's population increase by 25 percent.[32] Nationwide, African Americans were demanding the more equitable society for which they had fought. The state passed antidiscrimination legislation after the war: the Fair Employment Practices Law in 1949, the Vocational School Law (providing equal access to vocational training) and an end to the ban on intermarriage in 1951, and the Public Accommodations Law in 1953.[33] But serious deficiencies remained.

Brown vs. Board of Education
On May 17, 1954, the U.S. Supreme Court
decided unanimously that racial segregation
was illegal; it overturned the 1896 Plessy vs. Ferguson
decision (sidebar, p. 23).

Lawyers for the NAACP argued in a 1953 class action
suit on behalf of Linda Brown and other students that
the Topeka, Kansas, Board of Education was discriminat-
ing against the children by making them go to segregated
schools. The federal district court that heard the case
ruled in favor of the board of education on the grounds
that school facilities were of basically equal quality. The
NAACP appealed directly to the Supreme Court. (The
lead attorney presenting the argument for the plaintiff,
Thurgood Marshall, was appointed to the court by Presi-
dent Lyndon Johnson in 1967.)

After the court heard arguments, Chief Justice Earl
Warren worked and reworked an opinion that all the
justices would agree with. He knew that nothing less than
unanimity would do in relation to such an important
national issue.[34]

COLORED WOMAN PAYS HER MITE

Contributions to Hospital Fund Not Confined to Wealthy Class

She is a colored woman, and not making very high wages by doing washing and scrubbing for others. But she could afford to invest $250 of her little savings, by putting that much in the new Salem hospital fund, so the good old soul did not wait for a committee to call at her humble home, but yesterday afternoon walked into the headquarters at Commercial and State streets and handed in her mite, on the principle that it would help some poor wounded soldier back from the front, to have a leg mended, or an arm patched up.

An early twentieth-century act of generosity, a large donation by an anonymous elderly "colored woman" to the Salem Hospital (pictured below in 1920), was recognized in this 1917 article in the Statesman.

9

Close-up:
Carrie Halsell
Ward

Carrie Halsell's graduation portrait in the Oregon Agricultural College yearbook, *The Beaver*

Carrie Woodson Beatrice Halsell Ward is the first known African American student to have graduated from Oregon State University (then called Oregon Agricultural College—OAC). She earned her bachelor of science degree in commerce in 1926.

The Salem Years

Carrie was born in Boulder, Colorado, on October 26, 1903, the third of six children of William and Bessie Halsell. The family moved to Salem around 1912, William having taken a job with the railroad. He also worked in the orchards and harvested timber and was variously listed in Salem city directories as a janitor, laborer, and farmer between 1913 and 1917.

By 1921 Carrie's father had become a shopkeeper on State Street. That year he ran an ad in the directory, one that clearly reflected an entrepreneurial spirit:

Halsell, WJ (Bessie M) Cigars and Tobacco, Periodicals, Confectionery, Ladies' and Gentlemen's Shoe Shining Parlors, The Place That Pleases Everybody, 383 State opposite The Spa.

Carrie and her two older siblings, Agnes (Aggie) and Jesse, attended Salem High School, and the range of their activities was remarkable. *The Clarion*, the school's yearbook, shows that Aggie's hobby was music, that she was the piano

Carrie Halsell's Salem High School yearbook portrait, 1921

accompanist for a school musical, and that she wrote a play. She was also in the glee club, the girls' club, and the Latin club. (A portrait believed to be of Agnes is on p. 227.) Jesse played football, was sergeant at arms of the sports club, and played violin in the orchestra. In 1918 he appeared in a play called *The First Lady of the Land;* the caption of a photo of the production reads in part, "Jesse Halsell as the cook lent an atmosphere of reality." Carrie, an honor roll student, listed among her school activities glee club, girls' club, girls' reserve, commercial club, and typewriting contests. For her hobby, she wrote, "Books—school books excluded."

In 1922 Charles Maxwell, another black merchant with a shop on the same block as the Halsells' business, received a

The two black students in this early 1920s class picture from Salem High School are believed to be Jesse and Aggie Halsell

threatening letter from the KKK (see chapter 8). Whether the Halsells received a similar letter is not known, but even if they did not, it is hard to imagine that the news of such a letter escaped their notice. Whether in reaction to this incident or for entirely different reasons, the family moved to Portland and appeared in city directories there from about 1922 until 1926.

Incidentally, a Chrystalee Maxwell, believed to be Charles's daughter, appears in the 1928 *Clarion*. Like Carrie, she participated in several school activities including Latin club and the girls' league.

Oregon Agricultural College

Carrie's OAC transcripts show that she took a variety of business, accounting, and secretarial courses, as well as history, geology, education, literature, and both French and Spanish.

Although women students from 1922 through 1926 were expected to live in on-campus residences, Carrie always lived off campus. We doubt that this was by choice; it is more likely that she was denied housing in the all-white women's residence hall. She would only be allowed to live there, school officials indicated, if there were another black student with whom she could share a room.

Another possible sign of the entrenched prejudice of the time is that the requirement for female students to take nine credits of physical education was waived in Carrie's case, substituted with nine hours of French. We will never know for certain whether this was Carrie's choice or the school's, but it would not be surprising if mixing races in the shower was farther than school administrators were prepared to go.

Following her graduation from OAC in 1926, Carrie moved back into her parents' home in Portland and searched for work. Because job opportunities for blacks at the time were extremely limited, we find this well-educated and talented woman working as a housekeeper for the Meier and Frank department store. (It is worth noting that nearly forty years later in 1964, the same job with the same small chain of stores was the only one available to a new black female immigrant to the region, Claudia Thompson—see p. 200.)

A Career in Higher Education

In late 1926 or early 1927, Carrie moved to Virginia. Beginning in September 1927 she was employed at Virginia Normal and Industrial Institute (now Virginia State University), a

Carrie Halsell Ward in the 1930s

historically black college in Petersburg, first as an assistant to the registrar and later as an instructor of business education. In 1929 she helped establish the Alpha Eta chapter of Delta Sigma Theta sorority, one of the historic "divine nine" black sororities and fraternities.

While at Virginia Normal, Carrie met Louis Morris Ward, and in 1932 moved with him to his home state of Oklahoma, where the two were married. Both took teaching positions there at separate institutions. In 1935 the couple moved to South Carolina, and Louis joined the faculty at the College of Agriculture at South Carolina State College (now University).

There was a strict policy against spouses working at the same institution, so Carrie was not able to teach there until after the end of World War II when the policy was changed. In 1945 she accepted a faculty position in business administration, teaching such courses as shorthand, typing, business communication, and secretarial procedures. She also served as faculty advisor to Iota Phi Lambda sorority. During the summers she worked on her graduate studies, and in 1949 received a master's degree in business administration from New York University.

Carrie was active in service organizations and at church, and she and her husband enjoyed cooking and entertaining, often inviting students to their home. They also hosted card parties; according to family, they "probably owned at least four hundred decks of cards."

Apparently Carrie became estranged from her own family at some point. Friends and her husband's family members knew little of the Halsell family, except for the mention of a sister. Many did not know Carrie's maiden name, and it was not listed in her obituary. We do not know what happened to her parents, who had moved to San Francisco by 1930, to Agnes and Jesse, or to her other siblings, Minnie, Godfrey, and Jewel.

Through family members and friends we can glimpse Carrie Halsell Ward as a person: "organized and meticulous, expected her students to put the dot precisely over the 'i'"; "a quiet person, very caring, could draw friends unto her"; "very quiet and reserved, had a real love of children, exem-

Halsell Hall at Oregon State University, dedicated 2002

plary character ... the epitome of finer womanhood."

In addition to her own educational achievements, Carrie Halsell Ward's accomplishments were many. She spent most of her thirty-year career teaching at historically black colleges, helping other black Americans achieve the education they needed at a time when much of America was trying to hold them back. She understood the importance of peer support, which led her to her work with sororities. She served her church through leadership positions and served her community in numerous ways, including as Worthy Matron of the Eastern Star and as an officer of the American Association of University Women.

Louis died in 1974. Carrie Halsell Ward died at her home in Orangeburg, South Carolina, in 1989 at the age of eighty-five while carrying groceries from her car to her kitchen.

The Naming of Halsell Hall

In 2002, eighty years after Carrie Halsell enrolled as a student at OAC, a residence hall was named after her, bearing the alliterative name Halsell Hall. Carrie was chosen because she fit the four criteria that both students and housing staff had established for choosing a person to honor: she exemplified the university mission of student success, especially because she overcame barriers in order to achieve it; she was a member of an underrepresented group relative to those whose names appeared on other campus buildings—predominantly white, wealthy men; she had made community service a significant part of her life; and she was a pioneer, a "first." In addition, the students who were involved in the name search wanted the residence hall to be named for a student. In the end, those who researched her life concluded that no one could have fit the criteria better than Carrie Halsell.

Thanks to Terri Tower and Laurie Bridges for their research, undertaken for the purpose of choosing the name of the new residence hall at Oregon State University in 2002.

10

Close-up: William Tebeau

L ongtime Salem resident William Tebeau (pro-
nounced tee-bow) made history in 1948 in nearby
Corvallis, becoming the first male African American
student to graduate from Oregon State College (later
Oregon State University). Achieving this distinction had not been his aim, however. He was simply
focused on getting a degree in engineering, a goal he
had harbored since childhood while growing up in
Baker City, Oregon.

Tebeau's father worked as a janitor in Baker City; his mother
was a housewife. His grandparents, John and Malinda Tebeau, were children of former slaves who had escaped from
the South. John and Malinda arrived in Baker County on the
Union Pacific Railway in 1885, having been escorted from
their first choice of a place to settle—Mountain Home, Idaho—by its citizens, who had no intention of letting blacks live
there. So instead, just inside Baker County in the railroad town
of Huntington, the couple set up a business selling food to
travelers.

After John died, Malinda—who claimed to be the first
married black woman to live in eastern Oregon—moved her
then seven children to Baker City. Later, an African American
family of cowboys and rodeo performers, the Spearmans, arrived in town. Two marriages between the Spearmans and the
Tebeaus ensued, including that of William's parents.

A young man determined to succeed

Discrimination and racial tension were rife when William was growing up. The Ku Klux Klan was active in the community, as in many other areas of Oregon at the time, and Tebeau recalls being refused service at a local restaurant. He had made many friends in the town, however, and they immediately mobilized to boycott the business. This led to a sudden change of heart on the part of the owner, who apologized to the Tebeau family.

William in his OSC marching
band uniform

Despite the strains in race relations, Tebeau considers himself lucky to have grown up in Baker City and graduated from high school there in 1943. He describes it this way: "It was the best thing that ever happened to me. I had excellent teachers, and that really helped me when I got to college." In fact, he was able to skip his first term of writing courses at OSC because his exam scores were so high.

Tebeau's interests ranged beyond the technical. The prod-

William Tebeau and Arthur Bollinger at the
Oregon Highway Department, 1965

uct of a musical family, he was a musician of some accom-
plishment himself, playing violin and then trumpet in high
school. He and his friends in Baker City formed a dance band
that toured eastern Oregon, and during World War II, he and
a close friend played taps for fallen soldiers. When he got to
Corvallis, he played both in the Oregon State band and for a
studio band at the college's radio station, KOAC. Then, while
at the highway department, Tebeau, an Eagle Scout, helped
set up the Boy Scout Drum and Bugle Corps. Later, he would
work with the Flamingo Drum and Bugle Corps in Salem.

Tebeau's arrival at OSC in 1948, a full decade before fair
housing laws were passed, posed a dilemma for the college.

Housing discrimination was overt at the time: it was common for deeds to contain language prohibiting non-Caucasians from inhabiting a home unless they were servants. Tebeau had not specified his race on his college application, and when the new student came to the attention of Ulysses G. Dubach, the school's dean of men, Dubach had an awkward situation on his hands. He informed Tebeau that the school had no accommodations for him. Therefore, the dean suggested, perhaps the University of Oregon would be a better fit.

But the young Tebeau was not to be deterred. "Nobody else had engineering at the time," he would tell the Salem *Statesman Journal* sixty years later. "Fortunately, there were people in Corvallis who heard about my problem and helped out." One such person was Alma Hamer, the owner of a boarding house. She gave Tebeau his meals in exchange for his help in the kitchen, and found work for him at a fraternity next door; Tebeau tended the building's furnace in exchange for a room in its basement. Once again, we see in Tebeau's life an example of whites balking at the discriminatory practices aimed his way.

For his part, Tebeau doesn't dwell on the racism of his college years. He simply says of the time, "The people were good to me."

The people of Corvallis and OSC may have supported him, but after he graduated, Tebeau faced the stark reality that there were no job opportunities for black chemical engineers in the Pacific Northwest. He received some offers from back east and in Oklahoma and Texas, but none appealed to him. So he decided to return to Baker City and study on his own to become a licensed civil engineer, and soon he was hired to work for the highway department there. "When I decided not to follow a career in chemical engineering, I

William being honored for his years of work in Scouting

returned to Baker City and took a job as an engineering aide with the highway department. I didn't tell them I had a college degree, and I performed the most basic jobs while continuing to study for a civil engineer's license," he told OSU's alumni magazine. Thus began a thirty-six-year civil engineering career during which he worked on construction, surveying, and planning. He went on to describe the philosophy that has guided him: "Everyone wants to start out at the top, but I think they should start at the bottom and work their way up. It's the only way you can really know what's going on with the people who work for you. ... In my case, it made it easier for me to get along with people and to help them so they could do a better job."

Among Tebeau's proudest achievements is his work at

VICTOR ATIYEH
GOVERNOR

OFFICE OF THE GOVERNOR
STATE CAPITOL
SALEM 97310

December 31, 1984

Mr. William H. Tebeau
1146 38th NE
Salem, Oregon 97301

Please let me add my warmest congratulations to those of your
co-workers and friends as you complete your 36-year career with
the State Highway Division providing quality highways. I can
think of no finer service than public service and you have
performed it with distinction.

You have the gratitude of all Oregonians. Best wishes for the
greatest personal fulfillment in your well-earned retirement
years.

Sincerely,

Victor Atiyeh
Governor

VA:sl

Congratulations and thanks from Governor Atiyeh upon William's
retirement in 1984

Chemeketa Community College. He was a part-time instructor there for many years, dating back to 1957 when the school
was known as Salem Technical and Vocational Community

College. "He probably taught half the people at ODOT," says Cheri Tebeau-Harrell, his oldest daughter. "Everybody at ODOT knew Dad."

William Tebeau has never boasted about his singular pioneering achievement as the first black man to graduate from what is now OSU. Family and friends—even his wife of sixty years, Genevieve, whom he met in Baker City after college—were not even aware of it until recently. "I don't broadcast anything like that," he says. "I wasn't even concerned with history."

Information for this chapter came primarily from two sources: the December 2003 Oregon Stater, *OSU's alumni magazine, and a December 4, 2008, article in the* Statesman Journal.

11

The Later Twentieth Century and Beyond

March 8, 1957: rock 'n' roll comes to Salem. A poster promoting an all-star rock concert at South Salem High School.

While *Brown vs. Board* was a landmark decision, its impact was not immediately felt in Oregon. The African American citizens of Marion and Polk counties continued working to strengthen their community and fight for their rights. They faced many forms of discrimination: a greater likelihood of police harassment than protection; limited employment opportunities; and discrimination in housing, both in purchasing and renting.

Discrimination in Salem: A Typical Case

The *Statesman* of April 23, 1964, contained an article titled "Negro Couple Decides to Accept Salem Apartment." A landlord had refused to rent an apartment to Mr. and Mrs. Compton T. McKenzie. The McKenzies filed a lawsuit in Marion County Circuit Court alleging racial discrimination. Although the landlord had signed a conciliation agreement stating that he would rent the first available apartment to the McKenzies, he later reneged. The State of Oregon took the case to court: the first test of its anti-discrimination laws.[1] Midway through the trial, the landlord apparently had a change of heart. According to the *Statesman,* he "said the refusal to provide the apartment was due to a mix-up and he agreed ... to rent to McKenzie, providing McKenzie still wanted the apartment." The McKenzies accepted the offer.

Incidents like this, in which individuals and families had

Major Civil Rights Legislation and Court Decisions of the 1960s

In 1963, President Kennedy called on Congress to enact legislation protecting the rights of African Americans. After his death, President Johnson took up the cause and successfully mobilized national public opinion to get Congress to act. It took months of maneuvering to overcome opposition by Southern congressmen and senators, but the Civil Rights Act reached Johnson's desk in July 1964.

The act outlawed segregation in schools, jobs, and public accommodations, and banned long-used practices of voter suppression that had kept African Americans from exercising their rights and their political power, especially in the South. Now blacks and others struggling for freedom and equality had the law on their side everywhere in America.[2]

The Voting Rights Act of 1965 closely followed the language of the Fifteenth Amendment, which state officials had not consistently enforced. It prohibited states from imposing qualifications or prerequisites for voting based on race or color.[3]

The Twenty-fourth Amendment (ratified in 1964) prohibited poll taxes in federal elections. In 1966, the Supreme Court's Harper vs. Virginia Board of Elections *decision declared the tax unconstitutional under the equal protection clause of the Fourteenth Amendment and outlawed it in state elections as well.*[4]

to independently invest much time and expense to gain fair treatment, pointed to the need for an organized effort. The Salem chapter of the National Association for the Advancement of Colored People (NAACP) arose in response to this need.

The NAACP

The history of Salem's NAACP is one of chartering and re-chartering, beginning with the establishment of its first charter on July 2, 1970. The charter was revoked in 1971 for reasons unknown to us.

On January 16, 1973, Paul Golliday, a black resident and landowner in Aumsville, requested the assistance of the Corvallis branch of the NAACP. On February 27, 1974, Salem resident Chalmers Jones asked the Corvallis chapter for help in reestablishing the Salem branch. Corvallis chapter president Calvin O. L. Henry remembers assisting Jones in filing an application with the national office.

The organizers didn't wait for the paperwork to clear before acting. While rechartering was in the works, the Corvallis NAACP established a Salem subcommittee with temporary officers: Chalmers Jones, president; Jan Baptiste, vice president; Sharon Walker, secretary; and Marc Winters, treasurer. Calvin Henry worked diligently and closely with local citizens to address their issues.

In July 1974, a charter was granted that conferred the full rights and privileges of a unit of the organization. On July 30, Salem held elections for its officers and executive committee, and Jan Baptiste was elected president.

Over the years, the Salem chapter has gone through re-chartering several times as the people most active in it have moved on to other endeavors. Its presidential leadership has included Jackie Winters, David Burgess, Gwen

CHARTER

TO THE

MEMERS OF THE

Salem, Oregon Branch

OF THE

National Association for the Advancement of Colored People

GREETING:

Your Application for Admission to the

NATIONAL ASSOCIATION FOR THE ADVANCEMENT
OF COLORED PEOPLE

has been passed upon by the Board of Directors of the Association at its Meeting on
July 2, 1970 , and granted, and this charter is therefore issued to you.
Your organization is now enrolled as a Branch of the Association.

This Charter is granted on the condition that your organization will endeavor
to the best of its ability to cooperate with the National Association for the Advancement of
Colored People in furtherance of the Association's object, namely:

*"To uplift the colored men and women of this country by securing to them the full
enjoyment of their rights as citizens, justice in all courts, and equality of
opportunity everywhere."*

The Board of Directors reserves the right to suspend or revoke this Charter at any time the
Board shall deem it for the best interest of the Association.

Dated at New York this **2nd** Day of **July**, 1970

_____
Chairman of the Board

_____
Secretary

The Salem NAACP's charter, issued by the national office in 1970

Carr, James Ramsey, Bill Isabel, A. J. Talley, Lemuel Wade, Ted Envela, Sheryl Dash, Gregg Peterson, and today Benny Williams. It has worked closely with the Salem Human Rights Commission, a strong voice for the civil rights of Salem's citizens that achieved pioneering work in the area of housing.

A major focus of the chapter has been to recognize the achievements of prominent Oregonians in the area of civil rights. The chapter has also worked with a group of black inmates at Oregon State Penitentiary and has conducted an outreach program for youth in the community. The chapter of today still holds a recognition event and administers a youth program. To support its efforts and financial needs, it hosts membership drives and an annual Freedom Fund Banquet.

Oregon Northwest Black Pioneers

The Oregon Northwest Black Pioneers (ONWBP) is an all-volunteer nonprofit organization based in Salem. It was founded in 1993 with the mission of recognizing and commemorating the contributions of African Americans in the historical development of Oregon, and educating all Oregonians about that history. The organization was inactive from 1996 to 2004; at that point, new leadership emerged to resume its programs, including research and exhibits, scholarships, and youth development.

Led by an active board of directors, ONWBP works with community volunteers and confers with academic consultants and historical organizations to do research, compile historical information, and present its findings through oral presentations, exhibits, and publications. Since 2004, ONWBP has provided a variety of Oregon black history presentations to historical organizations, colleges, schools, civic clubs, and governmental agencies, primarily around the mid-Willamette Valley and Portland. In addition, it has provided exhibits in such venues as the Reed Opera House and Willamette Heritage Center in Salem, the Independence Heritage Museum, and in 2011, the Oregon Historical Society's Oregon History Museum in Portland with its exhibition, "Perseverance: Black Pioneers in Oregon's Early History."

In 2009 the Marion County Historical Society honored ONWBP with its David Duniway Award for Historic Preservation "in recognition of their many years of research, writing, teaching, documentation and preservation of the African American experience and contribution to the history of Marion County and Oregon."

In 2010 the Oregon Assembly for Black Affairs presented the OABA Education Award to the organization "for their outstanding use of education as a tool for change on behalf of Black Oregonians by researching and collecting historical information, documents and artifacts about the contribution of African Americans in the development of Oregon."

In 2011 ONWBP was a recipient of the American Heritage Award from *American Legacy: The Magazine of African American History and Culture* for "service, passion and dedication to the preservation of African American history and culture."

In 2009 ONWBP became the founding organization for another nonprofit to plan and build an Oregon African American museum. Early development work in this effort has progressed well, and a strategic plan to move this project forward is in the works. Recently, both groups have agreed to merge under one board of trustees and look forward to the day when the museum becomes a reality.

Churchgoing in Salem

Salem's earliest African American residents, arriving in the mid-1800s, were for the most part not welcome in white churches. There were two notable exceptions: the First Congregational Church led by Reverend Obed Dickinson (see chapter 5) and the First Methodist Church. We find no evidence that blacks were allowed to attend any other churches with whites until the 1920s, when the Salvation Army welcomed Annie Smith (see p. 99). This is the last information we have on black churchgoing in Salem until the 1960s. As of that decade, we know that some blacks were traveling to Portland to attend historically black churches. We do not know when this practice began, but it continues today.

Also in the 1960s, as blacks persevered in making Salem their home despite white antipathy, they banded together in small worship communities. These were largely made up of migrant farmworking families who had decided to settle here; the earliest known predominately black churches in Marion and Polk counties were of this kind.

Pastor Gussie Brown of the State Street Church of God gives us a window into one such church, though it was not the first she attended in the area. She recalls coming to Salem from Georgia to live with her sister in 1969 and initially joining the Free Church of God in Christ in Jesus Name under the leadership of Reverend Lawrence Clark. Worshippers met at his Church Street home on Saturdays. This church survives today, presently located on Lake Labish Road and now under the leadership of Evangelist Albertha Hunt.

A Country Church in Independence

Sister Gussie, who preferred Sunday services, learned of a nondenominational church in Independence that met in a

Pastor Gussie Brown

barn just off Highway 99, and this became her new worship community. It was founded by Elder Leslie and Marie Buckley sometime in the late 1960s. Most of its congregation were farm workers from Arizona who lived in and around Independence and knew each other from working together. Pastor Gussie remembers that there were "great services, like the old times in the south, with lots of singing, sometimes with guitars and drums."[5] There was even a Sunday school for the children. As she recalls, no whites attended the services.

State Street Church of God, 1750 State Street NE

There were no racial incidents connected with the church. However, in 1971, a gas leak caused an explosion in the barn-church. The Buckleys were both injured, but recovered fully. The barn was repaired, and worship continued.

Moving to Town
In 1973, Bishop Willie Vaughn from the Church of God in Seattle visited the services and invited the church to join the Church of God denomination. The congregation agreed, left the barn, and rented space for its services—first in West Salem and then downtown—while the Buckleys and Bishop Vaughn looked for a permanent home. In 1973, the State Street Baptist

Church sold one of its buildings on that street to the Church of God denomination, and worship began there.

From 1973 to 1991 there was a succession of nine pastors, most of whom commuted from outside Salem. During those years, Sister Gussie continued to worship and serve this church as a Sunday school teacher and superintendent. In 1993, when Pastor Lee Martin moved to Texas, Sister Gussie was asked to serve as interim pastor, and in 1998 she officially became permanent pastor, a position she holds to this day. Pastor Gussie Brown is the only black female pastor of the Church of God in the Pacific Northwest. Her State Street congregation now includes both blacks and whites.

Salem Mission

Another church took root in Salem during the same period. The story of Salem Mission Faith Ministries begins with Arthur Shankle in 1953. After serving in the army, he came to Eugene, Oregon, to visit his sister. He remembers not liking Oregon at first, and with good reason. At that time there were few blacks in Eugene and most lived in a flood area called Glenwood. They had no utilities or sewers, and they had to carry in water from the sewer station. Although he found no Jim Crow signs posted in town, there was little work for blacks except menial labor and a few railroad jobs. And blacks, he recalls, were not allowed to stay at hotels in the area.[6]

Arthur attended church with his sister and began to feel called to ministry. He gave his life to the Lord in 1953 and became licensed to preach at the Church of God in Christ in 1965. He founded Bethel Temple in Eugene the same year.

While at a church service in Portland, he met two women from Salem who had been regularly traveling there to attend church. He was touched by their faithfulness and com-

The Salem Mission Faith Ministries Church on Pringle Street

mitment, and together they began discussing the possibility of starting a church in Salem. The fruit of their discussions was the Salem Mission, founded in 1976. In the fall of that year, after a two-month search for a place to meet, the congregation began worshipping at the YWCA on State Street. In 1980, they found suitable property for a permanent home on Pringle Road, at a bend of the road in what is presently a residential area of South Salem that grew up around them. The first service was held in 1981.

Over the years, Reverend Shankle has become Bishop Shankle, and he alternates morning and evening services between the Salem Mission and Bethel Temple in Eugene.

Pauline Memorial
On a Thursday night in August 1972, a small group gathered in Portland in the home of Reverends Odell and

The Pauline Memorial AME Zion Church on Sunnyview Road

Nellie Thompson to begin organizing a new African Method-ist Episcopal (AME) Zion Church to be located in Salem. They decided to name the church in memory of Reverend Odell's mother, Pauline. The first service was held on September 2 in the dining room of the new ministers.

The tiny congregation was determined to move to Salem, and in the days that followed, the Thompsons made many trips there, seeking interested people, looking for a location, and getting ideas for their new church. On October 15, 1972, while still pursuing a permanent location, parishioners held their first service at Grant Elementary School on Broadway. After several months they found a place on Sunnyview Road. On April 1, 1973, they erected a sign on the property.

During the Easter season of 1976, on April 14, arson de-stroyed the edifice. "Black church strives to rebuild from ash-es of 'suspicious' fire" read the headline in the *Statesman* (the paper would change its name to *Statesman Journal* in 1980).

According to the article that followed, a prayer meeting had been interrupted on that day by "three abusive white youths." Hours later, the church burst into flames. Marion County Fire Department officials believed the fire to be of "suspicious origin," but no one was ever charged with the crime of arson.

After the fire, the Thompsons struggled to raise funds to rebuild the church while the congregation, which had dropped from fifty or sixty before the fire to around twenty, met in a room at the Salem First Methodist Church. Although there were concerns about rebuilding in Salem and some opposition to doing so, construction began in 1981. While the work was in progress, the congregation worshipped in local homes and at other locations including the First United Methodist Church on State Street and the YMCA on Court Street. Finally, on December 18, 1983, the group returned to its own building. The edifice was rededicated on January 29, 1984, and new life began for Pauline Memorial AME Zion Church.

In 1989 the Reverends Thompson received approval to take a leave from this ministry and were appointed to positions in other AME Zion churches in Oregon. Reverend Joyce Smith was appointed as pastor of Pauline in July 1989 and continued to serve in that capacity until 2009, when she left to accept a ministry position in Vancouver, Washington. During her tenure at Pauline, the church grew, adding more property and a modular building. It became very active in the Salem community, coordinating an annual Dr. Martin Luther King Jr. worship service with other churches and instituting the Reverend Nellie Thompson/Dorothy Patch Scholarship Awards. It also initiated a weekly community food bank and became recognized in the greater Salem community for its leadership. Reverend Antoinette Rochelle was appointed pastor in 2009, and the church continues to flourish under her direction.

Other Black Churches
Since the 1970s, several other predominately black churches have been founded and continue to hold services. They include:

- Amazing Grace Outreach Ministries, led by Clark and Brenda Ellison
- Seed of Faith Christian Center, led by Reverend Wade Harris
- Trinity Prayer House, led by Reverend Ivan McCrae
- To God Be the Glory Ministries, led by Reverend Ronnie Brooks

In addition, several black ministers have come to Salem to serve other churches. They include pastors Dell and Brenda Johnson at Northgate Community Church and Joe Parker, assistant pastor at Word of Life Community Church.

Growing Acceptance
As Salem's acceptance of blacks attending churches across denominations has grown, some of the current black population of churchgoers have successfully found their place among predominately white churches throughout the city.

Salem in the 1970s and 1980s

A Search for Community
The 1970s and 1980s brought a new influx of African Americans to the Salem area. Many came from out of state. Some came to escape the hustle and bustle of large cities while others sought expanded job opportunities that resulted from affirmative action and diversity programs. Blacks were actively

recruited to Salem-area colleges, government agencies, and major corporations.

The Salem-Keizer School District expended great effort in recruiting black teachers and administrators to respond to an increase in black children in classrooms. This recruitment had mixed results; while it succeeded in bringing blacks to the area, they often did not stay in town for long, resulting in ongoing concerns between local blacks and the school district. There were several reasons for lack of retention: insufficient preparation and cultural competence among district employees, underestimating the importance of cultural support for new black employees, inadequate professional support systems, and an inability to address strong feelings of isolation. These same dynamics were at work in other public agencies and private companies. We can assume that this was the case with Willamette University's first black professor, William N. Powell. We find an article in the school's newspaper announcing his arrival in 1970, but he was gone shortly thereafter.

Many of the new transplants had come from urban areas where minorities were in great abundance. Moving to a place where blacks were such a small minority and there had been little contact between blacks and whites on either a professional or personal level created a difficult and complex situation. Most whites in Salem had never worked with or been supervised by blacks, let alone lived alongside them. It was inevitable that there would be episodes of ignorant, offensive remarks and, at times, open resistance.

The spouses and children of these black professionals found similar circumstances in their workplaces and schools. The children were especially impacted, suddenly thrust into circumstances where they might be the only black child in a classroom, or even an entire school. They were subjected to

"I've never before been afraid to walk down the streets..."

The October 4, 1968, Willamette Collegian, *the university's newspaper, contained an article about nine black students voicing their concerns to the Human Relations Board about isolation and prejudice. Their on-campus issues revolved around a lack of black students (only 1 percent of the student population, compared to 10 percent nationally), an absence of black faculty members, and a lack of black-centered curriculum, such as a black history course. A board member responded to the latter complaint by observing that there was no money to recruit any black professors and that white professors were not prepared to teach an adequate black history course.*

The black students suggested actively recruiting students in high schools with large black populations and more recognition and support for black-oriented courses and library books. Part of their aim was to educate whites in the community in hopes of counteracting prejudice on and off campus. The article went on to say:

> *All the black students agreed that Salem was a bigoted town and much of this attitude was present on campus; they cited instances of racist attacks at public restaurants and whites stopping their cars or jumping out after the blacks. This feeling was expressed by one black student about walking Salem streets at night: "I've never before in my life been afraid to walk down the streets ... it's hard for me to understand."*

taunting and stereotyping by white children who reflected their own experience or family history.

African American families who came to the area during this period of time could go for months without seeing another black face. Unlike cities with larger black populations, where one would often see black letter carriers walking the streets, police officers protecting the citizenry, or retail clerks working in the stores, Salem's black middle class appeared nonexistent.

There was no central location in the community where most blacks—or even significant numbers of them—lived. (This, incidentally, remains true today, though there are more blacks in the area overall.) Unless they worked for a company or agency that had hired other African Americans, blacks had no easy way to connect with others living in town. For many new arrivals, Salem, Oregon, meant culture shock.

Without the touchstone of a familiar cultural center, many African Americans felt isolated. New hires had good jobs—often management positions—and they found the community a good place to live in many respects, but for many, the lack of cultural and professional support as well as negative experiences with the white community soon became deterrents to staying. There was constant ebb and flow as people came and tried to make a go of it, then went in search of a better environment in which to work and raise their families.

Present-day residents who persevered recall that on those occasions when blacks ran into one another, they would try to strike up a conversation and get acquainted. One woman tells the story of the day she was driving down the street and saw a black pedestrian. She pulled over, got out of the car, and called out, "Hello!" A typical stream of questions followed as a conversation ensued: "Where do you live?

Where do you work? Where do you go to church?"

Some people solved the isolation problem by moving to Portland and commuting to their Salem jobs. In Portland they found a greater concentration of blacks and a stronger sense of belonging: there were cultural opportunities, predominantly black churches with large congregations, and familiar music and art. There were merchants accustomed to serving the needs of a black clientele.

People living in Salem and the surrounding communities didn't have such advantages, and sometimes it was the little things that seemed to take the greatest toll. There was no African American programming or music on the radio. There wasn't a single black barbershop or beauty shop in town, and white barbers and beauticians did not have the skills or experience black clients required. Getting a simple haircut could devour most of a day, beginning with an hour-long trip to Portland. Women couldn't find cosmetics to match their skin tone because there had never been a need for merchants to stock those colors before. Stores were willing to order such products, but low demand meant they might not reorder. Christmas cards and other greeting cards all bore white faces.

Fortunately, there have been changes in the intervening decades as the black population has grown. African Americans now have multiple options for hair styling and makeup. There are ethnic lines of greeting cards in the stores. Such simple, practical things are indications of community recognition and support.

White Attitudes and Lack of Familiarity
Many white residents who encountered blacks during this period literally had never seen a black person in the flesh before. As a result, they carried preconceptions into their in-

teractions that were often heavily influenced by the images they saw on TV: a confusing mix of star athletes and entertainers and gangster types—dope dealers and pimps. Simply put, the presence of black people was strange, and some whites were unable to adjust.

In the workplace, this manifested as resistance. Black managers had their hands full dealing with whites who suddenly had black superiors for the first time. Some whites weren't shy about expressing their discomfort with this idea: one black person working in the school system was offered the suggestion that she might be more comfortable working up in Portland with her "own kind." Other types of resistance were more subtle, though no less discernible to those who were the object of them. And these dynamics extended beyond the behavior of subordinates to others in the community from whom cooperation was needed in order to achieve success in one's position.

Whites sometimes expressed their ignorance in ways that were annoying at best and insulting or intimidating at worst. They asked blacks what kinds of food they ate. They assumed all African Americans in town knew each other: "Do you know so-and-so?" was a frequent opening question after introductions were made. Blacks were often confused with other black people who looked nothing like them. Whites even wanted to know what black hair felt like. In the late 1970s, one African American woman shopping at the mall with her two young daughters was approached by several people who wanted to touch the little girls' hair. She gathered her daughters and fled.

An interesting—and again, mixed—result of a white community attempting to adjust to and assimilate blacks was an ongoing campaign to recruit them to serve on commissions and committees. While positive in its intent, this was problematic. Many blacks were hesitant to speak for all blacks in the community or were concerned that they would be seen as "tokens." Many were simply uncomfortable with being at the leading edge of this kind of integration. This left a very small pool of blacks who were willing to participate; they found themselves on multiple committees, which led ultimately to burnout. Thus we see again the ebb and flow of black participation in the community's structure.

During this period it was easy to feel like an oddity, and there was also the feeling of being a suspect. African Americans might be followed around by store staff while shopping; this was especially common for families with young children and older boys (it was assumed that they came to steal). There were allegations of police harassment, particularly taking the form of being pulled over without cause while driving, commonly known as DWB (driving while black).

Reaching Out
In the late 1970s and early 1980s, members of the African American community reached out to black newcomers when they learned of them. They invited them to lunch. Some people organized dinner parties and potlucks in their homes in honor of new residents and invited all the blacks they knew. Later, these gatherings often took on the nature of professional networking, moving out of the home and into restaurants: the Black Angus, no longer in existence, was the site of some of these meetings. These gatherings usually brought suspicious stares from white patrons, who voiced concerns that "something is going on" or wondered if "something is being planned."

Parents, concerned that their children didn't see other black kids often enough, created informal opportunities for them to get together. They arranged visits to the zoo in Portland or took the kids to programs sponsored by black sororities or other social organizations there. In the early 1980s, working through the NAACP, parents held workshops for kids to help them get summer jobs. Through these activities and others, the black community created a mutual support system. In addition, individual families made oases of their homes, filling them with art and music that reminded them of their heritage and culture, creating a revitalizing atmosphere. For those African Americans who were determined to stay, it was strategies such as these that made Salem, Oregon, feel like home.

Coming to Terms with the Past

As the twentieth century closed, some of Oregon's political leaders deemed it high time to officially recognize the state's long history of racist policies. Two events are notable indicators of this willingness to look back without illusions.

1999: A Day of Acknowledgment

On April 22, 1999, former governor Mark Hatfield and former national NAACP chair Myrlie Evers-Williams chaired the Day of Acknowledgment ceremony in the state capitol; more than eight hundred people attended the event. Governor John Kitzhaber and legislative leaders signed a resolution that both houses of the state legislature had passed earlier that day.

The resolution admitted that Oregon's history had been "marred by racial discrimination, exclusion, bigotry, and great injustice towards people of color, including Native Americans, African Americans, Latinos, Chinese Americans, Japanese Americans and Pacific Islanders." It also recounted the 1849 legislation that forbade "Negroes and mulattos" to live in Oregon: a law that was not repealed until 1926.

Phil Keisling, Oregon's then secretary of state, is quoted as saying that it might have been the best thing to happen in the legislature that year.[7]

2002: *Measure 14 Passes*
One hundred forty-five years after Oregon's constitution was ratified, a joint legislative committee placed Measure 14 before the state's voters. It set out to remove obsolete racial references such as "white population," "free negroes," and "mulattos" that had been written into the original constitution.

The argument in support of the measure, written by (among others) Portland State University professor Darrell Millner, State Senator Avel Gordly, and State Representative Jackie Winters, included these words:

> The Oregon Constitution currently contains racial provisions that are in violation of the United States Constitution's equal protection clause under the 14th Amendment.
>
> The prohibited language is contained in obsolete sections of the Oregon Constitution that have either been amended or repealed. Allowing this prohibited and biased language to remain is hurtful as well as unconstitutional. It is time to put an unenlightened period of Oregon's history behind us and remove this language from the Constitution.[8]

The measure passed with a vote of 867, 901 for and 352,027 against.[9]

12

Close-up: Claudia Thompson

Nurse Thompson, 1967

Claudia Thompson was Salem's first African American nurse, joining the staff of Salem Hospital in 1966. Claudia came to Oregon as an agricultural worker, picking beans and berries, and decided to stay. We interviewed her about her journey to the area and what life was like for blacks here in the mid- to late 1960s.

Leaving the South

Claudia was born in Ozan, Arkansas, the fourth of Lee Davis and Rheola Sampson's fourteen children. The family left Arkansas in 1951 after an incident that made it clear racial tension had not only reached their town but had touched their family. On a day like any other, her young brother and a friend bicycled into town to sell newspapers. While walking down the street, they passed a white woman. Immediately, a white policeman confronted them, demanding to know why they hadn't stepped off the sidewalk to let the woman pass—something they had never been told to do before—and he shoved the friend. This was enough for Lee Davis Sampson: despite the fact that his wife didn't want to leave, he decided to get his family out of the area before the situation worsened.

Claudia's sister had already left for Ohio and was working for a black contractor picking tomatoes. The money was good compared to what the family had been making in Arkansas, and the contractor was willing to hire them to harvest crops

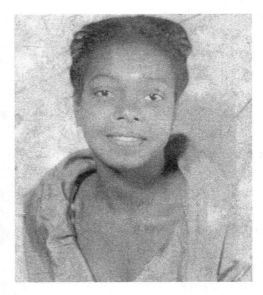

Claudia at Lincoln High School,
Washington, Arkansas

in Arizona. They left as quietly as they could, though as her father sold or gave away his wagon, his horses, and other belongings, word traveled: the Sampsons were leaving.

The family headed west on a flatbed truck with side boards and a tarp on top, taking with them as much food and as many blankets as they could stow in the space. They had no idea what conditions they would find as they journeyed toward their new home, and they wanted to be as prepared as possible.

Claudia recalls that they stopped every so often to take a break—until, that is, they reached Dallas, Texas. There, a banner over the highway coming into the city read, "The blacker the land, the whiter the people." Unbeknownst to Claudia, this came as no surprise to her father, who had already heard about racism, Texas style. They took no further breaks until they were well outside the city limits.

Once in Arizona, just outside Phoenix, the family arrived at the migrant camp to which they had been assigned. They were given two one-room cabins and put their belongings away, and then they all went straight to the cotton fields to pick. Their new life had begun.

Picking would take them to other parts of Arizona, and Claudia enjoyed the social life of the camps. When she enrolled in school, she found she was the only black child among around two thousand students at Glendale Union High School. At first, she didn't want to go back, and she tried every excuse she could think of to persuade her father to let her work and help her mother instead. He was unconvinced, adamant that all his children were going to get an education, so back to school she went. Claudia not only adjusted; she began to enjoy high school life. She recalls no instances of discrimination at all.

After graduation, a generous man her father was working for offered to loan him money to send Claudia to nursing school. Ironically, the future nurse declined. She had only been to a doctor once in her life and had never set foot in a hospital, and the thought of caring for the sick did not appeal to her at all. On this, Lee Davis Sampson relented: while getting an education was not negotiable, the field of study was.

In 1955, Claudia met Robert Lee Thompson, and they married "right out of the cotton field." Robert took her to meet his family in Texas, and they stayed there for a time, then returned to Arizona and resumed working in the fields.

Children came along, and she and Robert bought a little house near Scottsdale. He got a job delivering for a drug store, and she worked at the food counter.

Oregon: "Whole Trees Are Blooming"

In 1962, the family took a break for a few weeks and followed Claudia's parents to Oregon to pick crops. Claudia was immediately taken with the beauty of the area; she recalls asking her husband, "Can you believe whole trees are blooming?" In 1964, they came back to stay.

They arrived at a migrant camp at Parkdale in Hood River County late in the season and spent some time tending to berry plants. Then the contractor they were working for told them he was moving from that community at the foot of Mount Hood down to Independence for the winter—harsh weather was coming. He told them they could come along with him or go back to Arizona, as they wished. The Thompsons followed him, but after enduring the cold and rainy season in their single-walled migrant cabin, they decided to move to Salem. Claudia's sister and her husband were living there, and they stayed with them for a few months, looking for work but finding nothing.

Finally Claudia decided they had to face facts and ask for help so they could feed their children. "Let's go to the welfare department," she told her husband. "They help people." They soon learned, however, that there were some people the state welfare office would not help. Instead of offering assistance such as money for food and housing, the woman behind the counter told them the only help she could offer was a bus ticket to take the family back to Arizona.

Once again we find the thread of perseverance that runs throughout this book: Claudia did not take the welfare office

Close-up: Claudia Thompson

The Valley Migrant League, 1965

up on its offer—instead, she got mad. "I am not going," she told her husband. "I'm going to find some kind of work." They had been to the employment office many times before, finding nothing, but they went back. This time there was a job for Robert at a turkey processing plant in West Salem.

By this time Claudia had gained some experience as a nurse's aide, beginning in Phoenix. The man at the employment office gave her a card to show her prospective employer and sent her to Salem Hospital, then called Salem General. The receptionist took the card, looked at it, and handed it back, telling Claudia there were no openings. Back to the employment office and to the same clerk she went with her story of what had happened. "Well, let's just see," he said. He picked up the phone and called to ask whether the hospital was hiring nurse's aides. Yes, he was told immediately, they were.

Frustrated, the clerk gave her another card and sent her to the Meier and Frank department store, where she landed a job as a housekeeper. After working there for a short while, she remembers being called into co-owner Jerry Frank's office one day. He asked her how she was being treated, and she replied she was being treated very well. "We don't want any prejudice around here," she recalls Frank saying. "If there's any problem, you come to me."

Nursing

One of the men on staff at the employment office urged Claudia to pursue a career. He encouraged her to take an aptitude test at Salem Tech, now Chemeketa Community College. By this time President Johnson had signed the Manpower Act into law, and there were funds available to pay low-income and minority students' tuition. After reviewing her test results, the president of the college invited her to join its nursing program.

Completing the program was a tremendous challenge; her father was ill at the time, and her youngest children cried for her attention as she studied behind a closed door. Her father gave her strong encouragement, though, telling her he'd be in the front row at her graduation ceremony. Unfortunately, he would not live long enough to see that moment.

Armed now with her degree, Claudia returned to Salem Hospital. This time she was hired and worked there for nearly five years. Then she moved to Fairview Hospital, a state-run facility that paid higher wages. There, a combination of racial prejudice and jealously (she had gotten a job others who had worked there for years believed they deserved) resulted in some conflict. It culminated in an episode during which a woman called her the n-word. Claudia reported her cowork-

Claudia and other nurses, 1976

er, and their supervisor admonished the woman and made her apologize.

When Claudia was pregnant with her fourth child she decided to take a break from nursing. The family was living in a big farmhouse at the time, owned some cows, and had bought their son a horse. She wanted to live the country life with her family for a while.

It wasn't easy for blacks to find housing during this period; Claudia recalls widespread discrimination. When the family wanted to move out of her sister's house and was looking for a new place, they had their eye on one that was advertised, but when the landlady learned they were black, she maintained that the house was no longer for rent.

Eric, Bruce, Bob, and Claudette in their store, A-1 Tackle, 1984

Later, Claudia would serve on the human rights commission, and she recalls two young men calling her to complain that they had been turned down for a particular house on the basis of race. In an echo of her first experience with Salem Hospital and the clerk at the employment office, she called the property manager, disguised her voice, and asked if the place was for rent. Sure enough, it still was. It happened that the landlord's mother was sick and Claudia was caring for her. She told the landlord about the incident. He saw to it that the house went to the young men and asked her to tell him if she ever ran across similar problems.

In the mid- to late sixties, she recalls there were at least five or six African American families in Salem. Their entertainment consisted of visiting one another's homes, playing cards, listening to music, dancing, and having a few beers. Visiting bars was an iffy proposition, though. "Men just wanted to be men," she remembers. Her husband and nephews

Claudia and her mother, Granny Rheola Sampson,
2002

"would have a beer at a bar, but they always got called the
n-word. If I went anywhere with them, I made sure we went
to a restaurant instead so we wouldn't get into that situation."

Claudia recalls many incidents of intimidation, and some
of violence. Her children were chased off the road into a ditch
by white teenage boys in cars as they walked to school—this
happened more than once. Her eldest son received threaten-

ing calls when he was home alone after school and she and her husband were at work, the voice telling him to get out of town: "We don't want you Ns here." The calls only stopped when her husband stayed home from work in order to answer the phone himself. (She doesn't know what he said, but the calls stopped after that.) Claudia remembers that a retired man had a heart attack when some young white boys threw rocks through his window. The KKK burned crosses on her niece's lawn as the family slept one night, and on another night fired bullets into her bedroom. The Thompson family found unwelcome fliers in their mailbox more than once.

Claudia retired from Salem Hospital after more than thirty years of nursing. She still lives in Salem and can frequently be found at Pure Elegance, the beauty salon belonging to her daughter, Claudette.

Given the blatant racism and open hostility the Thompsons encountered, one might wonder why they stayed. For Claudia, the answer is easy: on the whole, she feels she has been treated well, and it's a beautiful place to live. "Mountains, ocean—you can take your pick. And we're big campers, fisherman, and deer hunters. We've camped every day we could since we've been here. I don't think there's any other place that can offer you this kind of beauty."

Artifacts from the Migrant Life

Black migrant workers returned to the Willamette Valley to pick crops season after season. One company they worked for was E. G. Fuson in Aumsville. Here are a few surviving items from the 1950s and 1960s.

Tickets crediting workers for pounds of produce they have picked

Children playing to the camera, 1962

May 27 - 63
Mr. E. G. Susan
Dear Sir

You said to drop you a line just before School Closes if we wanted our Same Cabin. We would like to have it again please. We hope to leave sometime around the middle of June. If its alright with, with you. If thats too Early to come, please let me Know thank you.

Pearlie Mae Evans

A letter arranging for work and lodging in the summer of 1963

An unidentified migrant family

13

Salem Today

The populations of Marion and Polk counties today total nearly four hundred thousand, of which fewer than 2 percent are African American. While some blacks have lived in this part of Oregon for many generations, most have migrated within the last fifty years. They came here for a variety of reasons: some were migrant workers who settled here; some responded to local recruiting efforts; some moved from urban areas in search of smaller communities; some took jobs in state and local government.

As has been mentioned, African Americans are not concentrated in a single geographic area of the two counties but are spread throughout the region. They are found in virtually all aspects of the counties' community life, including civic involvement, business, and the nonprofit world.

A list of contemporary "firsts"—the area's modern black pioneers—would be too long to publish. (We extend both apologies and gratitude to the many African Americans who have contributed to making history here but are unnamed in this book.) Instead we provide a few examples that show how life has changed for blacks here.

Salem Hospital, where a "colored woman" donated $250 in 1917 and Claudia Thompson became the first black nurse in the 1960s, has had as its legal counsel a black man, Jack Caynon.

Willie Richardson, who currently serves as board chair of

the Oregon Northwest Black Pioneers and the developing Oregon African American Museum, was elected to the board of Salem-Keizer School District, serving from 1987 to 1991.

Geraldine Hammond became the first African American principal of any school in Salem in 1976; the city's school system has named an elementary school after her. Cynthia Richardson served at McKay High School and was named principal of North Salem High in 2010, the first black principal of a high school in the city.

Dr. Cheryl Roberts was named president of Chemeketa Community College in 2007. She had previously held positions at South Seattle Community College, Seattle Central Community College, the University of Washington, and Lane Community College in Eugene.

Dr. F. Lee Pelton served as president of Willamette University for thirteen years until 2011. During his first year, Salem's *Statesman Journal* described Dr. Pelton as "an Ivy Leaguer in the land of Pendleton plaid shirts ... an East Coast intellectual with a Midwesterner's sensibilities ... a black man in a predominately white state, an academic in a CEO's role, a man of letters in a job that requires crunching the numbers, a man of faith in the largely unchurched Northwest." On May 14, 2011, the newspaper concluded an editorial with these words: "The community and the university has been blessed with Pelton's leadership. Boston is Pelton's intellectual home but we trust he will always regard Salem as his home away from home." The university plans to rename a building after Dr. Pelton.

Also leaving Willamette University in 2011 was Walter Robinson, who had earned a bachelor's degree in politics; he graduated as the university's first African American student body president. He served as a student representative on Willamette's board of trustees and was a member of the search

Above: Geraldine Hammond. Below: Geraldine Hammond Elementary School.

Jim Hill, Oregon state treasurer, state senator, and
state representative

committee to find Dr. Pelton's replacement.

In the political sphere, Jim Hill of Salem became the state
treasurer in 1992, the first African American elected to statewide office in Oregon. He had previously served in the Oregon State Senate from 1987 and the state's House of Representatives from 1983 to 1987. He ran for governor in 2002
and 2006.

Jackie Winters is currently in her fourth term as a state
senator from South Salem. Her family moved to Portland from
Topeka, Kansas, in 1941 and lived through the Vanport flood

Jackie Winters, businesswoman and
state senator

of 1948. Her public service dates back to 1959, with her work
at Oregon Health Services University and later on the staff
of the Portland Model Cities Program. She was appointed
ombudsman by Governor Victor Atiyeh in 1979. She was elected to the House of Representatives in 1998 and elected to the
state senate in 2002. She has lived in Salem for more than forty
years. In 1985 she opened the first Jackie's Ribs, which was
followed by three more restaurants in Salem and three fran-
chises. She has served on numerous boards and commissions
and has received many awards and recognitions.

Salem City Councilor Sheryl A. Thomas

In 2011 Sheryl A. Thomas was elected to the Salem City Council, the first African American to attain this office.

Salem's law enforcement and corrections departments have been served by pioneers such as Chalmers Jones, Hazel Hayes, Frank Thompson (the first black corrections superintendent), and Lonnie Jackson at the Oregon Youth Authority.

In the nonprofit sector, Gwen Carr served as board president of the YWCA Salem from 1998 to 2008 and served as interim executive director after the tenure of its first black CEO, Natalie Dunn. Jason Caldwell was operations director for the

Boys and Girls Club of Salem before joining the Salem-Keizer School District as a behavioral specialist. Marie Blevins Bradford has served many years as executive director of the Salem Riverfront Carousel.

Within the last few years new black businesses have emerged. A Time for Elegance, owned by Willie Richardson, evolved from a hat shop to a formalwear store. (Willie retired the business in 2010.) Claudette Fields, daughter of Claudia Thompson, opened Pure Elegance, a spacious hair salon and spa, in 2008. Brenda Warren owns Anise's On Broadway Hair.

Other black-owned businesses in Salem include Q's Corner Barbershop on High Street, Gregg Peterson's Broadway Café, and Just Bucket, owned by Willie Davis Jr., a successful excavating company for more than twenty-five years.

A Sampling of Black-owned Businesses in Salem

A Time for Elegance, Willie Richardson's formalwear store

Anise's on Broadway Hair Salon and Wig Boutique

Claudette Fields's hair salon and spa, Pure Elegance

Q's Corner Barber Shop on NE High Street

Broadway Café, owned by Gregg Peterson

Afterword

We come to the end of this book knowing full well that it really has no ending. Concerning those who have gone before, countless gaps and omissions remain; our research necessarily continues. And the black history of Marion and Polk counties continues to be made as new people arrive to settle in the area and long-time residents find new ways to contribute to their communities.

We invite you to help us in our efforts to obtain and convey a fuller picture of Oregon's African American history, and in extending this invitation we widen the lens to include the entire state. We have discovered black history in thirty counties—are there stories we have not yet heard about black settlement in the remaining ones? Can you help us find them? If we pull the threads of the profiles we are aware of, do they lead to even more African American Oregon history?

The Oregon Northwest Black Pioneers is presently laying the groundwork for the Oregon African American Museum, the purpose of which is to collect, preserve, interpret, and exhibit evidence of the African American experience in Oregon. This is a natural extension of the work we have done to date, and one that promises a new level of educational value. We welcome any information, photographs, or artifacts you may wish to contribute to this future statewide resource. And if you can identify any of the people who are listed in illustrations in this book as "unknown" or "unidentified," we'd greatly appreciate hearing from you.

As we close this book—an important addition to our shared body of knowledge—let us take a step back and look at the significance and value of ONWBP's work. What fuels the enthusiasm and commitment of our volunteers? Why do we expend such effort in research, publishing, and community outreach? Because we have found that the information we present is extremely important to the African American psyche in Oregon. And the reason it has such an impact is simple: it proves that we belong here. We have been here since before the wagon trains. We have lived all over the state, even in some of the most unexpected places. This history has meaning to Oregon's black citizens. It is welcome news for the adults who come to live here, and it is especially important for their children, to help connect them to their new home. It is also important to Oregon's citizens of all colors in that it bears witness to the historical diversity of the state.

As we have chronicled, if you are an African American living in Oregon, it can be all too easy to feel isolated absent the support of a large and visible black community. It can be easy to think of yourself as a kind of interloper. But when you are presented with undeniable evidence that people of your heritage have in fact been here for centuries and that their strength, courage, and perseverance have made life better for every generation to follow, you come to know that you are indeed a real Oregonian. You can make this place your home.

A Photo Gallery

The Cronise Collection

The portraits on the following seven pages are by Thomas Cronise, a photographer who took photos of many Salem residents, including these African Americans. Some of the photos here also appear in a book titled *The Art Perfected*. His collection is housed at the Oregon History Museum in Portland.

OrHi bb006949

Mr. T. C. King, 1893

W. G. Johnson of Salem, 1902

OrHi bb06952

OrHi bb06953

Miss S. E. Buford, 1917

Ruth Davidson, 1917

OrHi bb06954

OrHi bb06955

This is believed to be a portrait of Carrie Halsell's sister, Agnes, in 1918.

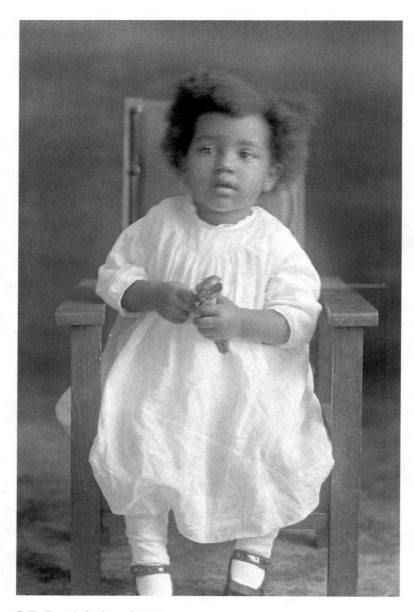

S. D. Paris's little girl, 1917

OrHi bb06956

OrHi bb06976

Mrs. L. C. Chambers

OrHi bb06977

Faces without names: an unidentified woman, from the Cronise collection. If you can identify her, please contact Oregon Northwest Black Pioneers.

OrHi bb007665

Mr. And Mrs. Owen L. Lynthecom and their son Owen

Tiger Engine Company hose team at the 1886 Firemen's Tourna-
ment in Salem. Photo from *History of the Salem, Oregon Fire Department: The Volunteer Era, 1857 to 1893* by John Wilkerson (Salem: Old
Time Bottle Publishing Company, 1976).

A black student in a Salem school, 1904

Herb Golliday Jr. in class, 1950

Faces without names: an unknown black player on the Woodburn High School basketball team, 1918. If you can identify him, please contact Oregon Northwest Black Pioneers.

A Timeline

1788: Marcus Lopius (Lopez) is the first person of African descent known to set foot in Oregon.

1803–06: York, William Clark's slave, explores the West with Lewis and Clark.

1823: Black mountain man Moses Harris comes west to help build forts and do fur trading; he will later guide several wagon trains to the region.

1843: The Cockstock Incident.

The provisional government's Organic Law restricts voting to "free white male descendants of white men 21 or older."

Rachel Belden moves to Oregon with her master, Daniel Delaney; they live east of Salem.

1844: Slavery is declared illegal in the Oregon Country. An exclusion law is passed, freeing slaves but requiring blacks to leave within three years. Its "lash law" provision is also passed but soon replaced by forced labor.

George Washington Bush goes north to escape the lash law.

1846: Oregon Treaty establishes the Oregon Country.

Jesse and Lindsay Applegate lead a wagon train to the Willamette Valley via the Applegate Trail.

1848: Territorial legislature replaces provisional government.

1849: Oregon passes a new exclusion law after the Whitman Massacre in Walla Walla.

Oregon becomes a territory August 14. Blacks living in Oregon are allowed to stay but new blacks are banned. Supporters of black residents in Portland present exemption petitions to the territorial government, which rejects them.

Ox driver Travis Johnson, slave of Philip Glover, arrives in Oregon.

1850: The Oregon Donation Land Law gives free land to "whites and half-breed Indians" in the territory while forbidding blacks to claim land.

1850 census: 207 blacks in Oregon; 9 in Marion County.

1851: Portland residents petition the legislature to exempt the Francis brothers from the exclusion law.

Jacob Vanderpool, an Oregon City saloon keeper, becomes the only person known to be evicted from Oregon Territory under the exclusion law.

John Scott drowns on his way back from the California gold fields.

1852: The Holmes family case: Robin Holmes sues Nathaniel Ford.

Obed Dickinson moves to Salem.

1853: Louis Southworth moves to Oregon with his master.

The Holmes ruling.

1854: The exclusion law under which Jacob Vanderpool was exiled is repealed.

Blacks and Indians are prohibited from testifying in any legal action brought by or against whites.

1855: A law is passed to deny citizenship to mixed-race males.

1857: A new exclusion law is added to the state constitution by popular vote. It forbids blacks to move into the territory or vote. It will not be repealed until 1926.

The *Dred Scott* decision: slavery is legal in U.S. territories.

1858: Oregon elects its first state officials: many, including the governor, are openly pro-slavery.

Hannah and Eliza Gorman buy property in Corvallis.

1859: On February 14, Oregon becomes the first state admitted to the Union with an exclusion law written into its state constitution.

1859: Louis Southworth makes enough money mining gold and playing his fiddle to buy his freedom.

1860s and 70s: School segregation in Portland, Pendleton, and Salem (1868–1874).

1860 census: Oregon total population 52,465; black population 128. Marion County total 7,088; black population 20; Salem black population 17.

1861: The Civil War begins. The pro-Southern Knights of the Golden Circle open chapters in many Oregon communities.

1862: State adopts a poll tax applying to blacks and other nonwhites; failure to pay is punishable by road-gang labor. The legislature bans marriage between whites and persons with a quarter or more of "Negro blood." Black people can serve as witnesses in court but not as jurors. Black children can attend schools in the state.

1863: Emancipation Proclamation.

Marriage of Richard Bogle and America Waldo, officiated by Obed Dickinson of the First Congregational Church.

1864: The Knights of the Golden Circle fall apart as inevitable Union victory becomes apparent.

1865: End of the Civil War. The state legislature passes the Thirteenth Amendment.

Jackson Bonter marries Mary Parks at Obed Dickinson's church.

Daniel Delaney is murdered by two white men posing as blacks.

1866: In a close vote, the state legislature ratifies the Fourteenth Amendment, which grants citizenship to blacks.

The state legislature passes a law expanding its ban on miscegenation: it outlaws marriage between whites and persons with a quarter or more of "Negro blood," Chinese, "Kanakas" (native Hawaiians), and Native Americans.

1867: Salem's "colored school" opens.

1868: Democratic-majority state legislature rescinds the previous legislature's ratification of the Fourteenth Amendment. The state legislature also passes "An Act to protect the owners of Fire Arms": a misleading name for a law making ownership of firearms illegal for all but white males over the age of sixteen.

Salem citizens celebrate at the Emancipation Jubilee.

1870: The Fifteenth Amendment, granting black men the right to vote (and superseding the state constitution's ban on black voting), is added to the U.S. Constitution while failing to pass in Oregon.

Census: Black population in Oregon 346; Marion County 62; Salem 50.

Louis Southworth moves to Buena Vista.

1872: William P. and Elizabeth Johnson adopt Rosetta Bonter.

1880 census: Black population in Oregon 487; Marion County 27.

1883: Unsuccessful attempt to amend the Oregon Constitution to remove its ban on black voting. Further attempts to remove language prohibiting blacks from voting are made in 1895, 1916, and 1927.

Statesman *pressman Hiram Gorman is replaced by a steam motor.*

A railroad from the East Coast to Portland is completed.

1887: Washington Territory ends its ban on interracial marriage.

1889: Washington becomes a state. Its constitution bans school segregation.

1890 census: Black population in Oregon 1,186; Marion County 139.

1892: John W. Jackson dies and is buried in Hayesville Cemetery.

1895: Annie Smith joins the Salvation Army in Salem.

1896: The *Plessy vs. Ferguson* decision: "separate but equal."

1897: California passes its first civil rights law.

1900 census: Oregon total population: 413,536; black population 1,105; Marion County 49; Salem 5.

1903: McCants Stewart becomes the first African American admitted to the Oregon state bar.

1905: The State Theater in Portland refuses to let Oliver Taylor sit in a box seat. He sues, loses in local court, appeals.

1906: McCants Stewart successfully argues Oliver Taylor's discrimination suit in the state supreme court.

Albert Bayless celebrates his eighty-seventh birthday.

1910 census: Oregon black population 1,492; Marion County 58; Salem 47.

1911: E. C. Atkinson wins his lawsuit against the Grand Opera House.

1914: The Portland chapter of the NAACP, the oldest continually chartered chapter west of the Mississippi River, is founded.

1916: Voters reject a proposed state constitutional amendment to end the ban on nonwhite voting (the Negro and Mulatto Suffrage Amendment).

1919: Effort begins to pass law making discrimination in public accommodations illegal. Such a law will pass in 1953.

1920s: The Ku Klux Klan attracts as many as thirty thousand members in Oregon.

1920 census: 2,144 blacks in Oregon; 72 in Marion County; 63 in Salem.

1922: Beatrice Morrow Cannady is the first African American woman admitted to the state bar.

Charles Maxwell receives a threatening letter from the KKK.

1924: The Oregon Real Estate Department adopts the National Association of Real Estate Boards' code of ethics to prevent blacks from buying houses in white neighborhoods.

1926: Oregon voters amend the state constitution to repeal the exclusion law from the state Bill of Rights.

Carrie Halsell becomes the first black graduate from Oregon Agricultural College (later OSU).

1927: Voters amend the Oregon State Constitution to allow "Negro, Chinaman and Mulatto suffrage."

1930 census: black population in Oregon 2,234; Marion County 63; Salem 58.

Miscegenation is declared a felony.

1932: John M. "Johnny" Jones, Salem caterer, dies, appx. eighty.

1937: Annie E. Smith, Salvation Army Ward Sergeant, dies.

1940 census: 2,565 blacks in Oregon; 57 in Marion County; 56 in Salem.

1941: U.S. enters World War II.

Ca. 1943: Willamette University student Mark Hatfield drives Paul Robeson to Portland because no hotel in Salem will serve him.

1948: William Tebeau graduates from Oregon State College (later OSU).

The Vanport flood.

1949: Legislature passes Fair Employment Practices Law.

1950 census: 11,259 blacks in Oregon; 138 in Marion County.

1951: Oregon repeals the law banning interracial marriages.

Auto insurance surcharges for nonwhites are ended.

A Timeline

Discrimination in vocational schools is banned.

1953: Legislature passes a public accommodations law.

1954: The *Brown vs. Board of Education* decision outlaws segregation.

1957: A state fair-housing law passes, applying to housing with five or more units.

1959: Oregon voters ratify the Fifteenth Amendment.

The state fair housing law is expanded to all sales and rentals.

1960 census: 18,133 blacks in Oregon; 216 in Marion County; 167 in Salem.

1961: Ban on discrimination by any place offering goods and services to the public.

1964: Congress passes the Civil Rights Act.

1965: Congress passes the Voting Rights Act.

1966: Claudia Thompson becomes Salem's first black nurse.

1967: U.S. Supreme Court declares bans on interracial marriage unconstitutional.

1970 census: 26,308 blacks in Oregon; 530 in Marion County; 349 in Salem.

Salem's first NAACP chapter is formed.

Willamette University hires its first black professor, William N. Powell.

1972: William McCoy, Democrat of Portland, becomes the first African American elected to the state legislature.

1973: The state ratifies the Fourteenth Amendment.

1976: Geraldine Hammond is named Salem's first African American school principal.

1980 census: 37,060 blacks in Oregon; 1,258 in Marion County; 1,225 in Salem.

1984: Margaret Carter, Democrat, is the first African American woman elected to the state legislature.

1985: The state legislature creates a civil rights division.

Martin Luther King Jr.'s birthday is declared a state holiday.

1990 census: 46,178 blacks in Oregon; 2,132 in Marion County; 1,632 in Salem.

1992: Jim Hill of Salem is elected Oregon state treasurer, the first African American elected to statewide office.

1993: Oregon Northwest Black Pioneers is formed.

1998: M. Lee Pelton is named president of Willamette University.

Jackie Winters becomes the first black Republican to be elected to the state legislature.

1999: Day of Acknowledgment.

2000 census: 56,662 blacks in Oregon; 2,539 in Marion County; 1,750 in Salem.

2002: Voters pass Measure 14, removing racial references from the state constitution.

2008: Barack Obama is elected the first African American president of the United States.

2010 census: 64,984 blacks in Oregon; 2,906 in Marion County; 2,801 in Salem. Polk County black population 394.

Sheryl A. Thomas becomes Salem's first black city councilor.

2011: The Oregon Northwest Black Pioneers and the Oregon African American Museum merge in order to focus on establishing a museum in Salem.

Illustration Credits

Cover photo: Marie (Mrs. Owen) Lynthecom, 1917. Courtesy of Oregon Historical Society (OHS) (OrHi bb06951)

4. Courtesy of Oregon Northwest Black Pioneers (ONWBP)

11. http://arcweb.sos.state.or.us/echoes/pics/6024.jpg

21 (top). Courtesy of Willamette Heritage Center *(Historic Marion)*

21 (bottom). Courtesy of ONWBP

28. Courtesy of Rick Stever

33. Courtesy of Meadowlark Publishing Services (MPS)

47. Courtesy of Benton County Historical Society

49, 51. Courtesy of MPS

56. Courtesy of OHS (OrHi bb06958)

66. Courtesy of OHS (OrHi 89474)

67. Courtesy of MPS

75. Courtesy of MPS

80. Courtesy of First Congregational Church

91. Courtesy of MPS

93. Courtesy of MPS

96–98, 100–01. Courtesy of MPS

105 (both). Courtesy of Willamette Heritage Center

108 (top). Courtesy of ONWBP

108 (bottom). Courtesy of MPS

112. Courtesy of MPS

115. Courtesy of OHS (OrHi 07000)

116, 117, 120, 123. Courtesy of MPS

124–25. Courtesy of Friends of Salem Pioneer Cemetery

128 (top). Courtesy of Virginia Green

128 (bottom). Courtesy of Willamette Heritage Center

130. Courtesy of Carole Smith

131. Courtesy of OHS (OrHi ba018361)

132. Courtesy of OHS (OrHi bb06959)

139. Courtesy of Carole Smith

140. Courtesy of OHS (OrHi bb002154)

143–44. Courtesy of David Rhoten and ONWBP

148 (top). Courtesy of the *Statesman Journal*

148 (bottom). Courtesy of Willamette Heritage Center

150. Courtesy of Oregon State University

152. Courtesy of North Salem High School

153. Courtesy of Willamette Heritage Center (MCHS 83.1.17)

155. Courtesy of Terri Tower

157. Courtesy of MPS

160–67. Courtesy of William Tebeau family

170. Courtesy of the *Statesman Journal*

174. Courtesy of ONWBP

178–79. Courtesy of Pastor Gussie Brown

181, 182. Courtesy of MPS

194–201. Courtesy of Claudia Thompson

202. Courtesy of Claudia Thompson and the *Statesman Journal*

203. Courtesy of Claudia Thompson

205–06. Courtesy of Gaius and Marcus Fuson and Louise Fuson Shepard

211 (top). Courtesy of Geraldine Hammond

211 (bottom). Courtesy of MPS

212. Courtesy of Jim Hill

213. Courtesy of Jackie Winters

214. Courtesy of Sheryl A. Thomas

216. Courtesy of ONWBP

217 (top). Courtesy of ONWBP

217 (bottom). Courtesy of Claudette Fields

218 (top). Courtesy of Q's Corner Barber Shop

218 (bottom). Courtesy of MPS

223. Courtesy of OHS (OrHi bb06949)

224. Courtesy of OHS (OrHi bb06952)

225. Courtesy of OHS (OrHi bb06953)

226. Courtesy of OHS (OrHi bb06954)

227. Courtesy of OHS (OrHi bb06955)

228. Courtesy of OHS (OrHi bb06956)

229. Courtesy of OHS (OrHi bb06976)

230. Courtesy of OHS (OrHi bb06977)

231. Courtesy of OHS (OrHi bb07665)

232. Courtesy of John Wilkerson

233 (top). Courtesy of Salem Public Library

233 (bottom). Courtesy of Willamette Heritage Center

234 (both). Courtesy of Woodburn Historical Museum

Notes

Chapter 1

1. www.blackpast.org/?q=perspectives/black-laws-oregon-1844-1857
2. Dick Pintarich, *Great and Minor Moments in Oregon History* (Portland: New Oregon Publishers), 2008, 285–86.
3. Melinda Jette, "The Cockstock Incident." *Oregon Historical Quarterly* 4-405-406. www.ohs.org/education/oregonhistory/historical_records/dspDocument.cfm?doc_ID=8931E17D-CDFA-0C0F-B2564A92A5334C96
4. Elizabeth McLagan, *A Peculiar Paradise: A History of Blacks in Oregon, 1788–1940* (Portland: Georgian Press, 1980), 19–20.
5. http://en.wikipedia.org/wiki/York_(explorer)
6. McLagan, *Peculiar Paradise,* 10.
7. www.historicoregoncity.org
8. Ibid.
9. www.drbilllong.com/CurrentEventsVIII/LandII.html
10. McLagan, *Peculiar Paradise,* 88–89.
11. www.oregonencyclopedia.org/entry/view/oregon_donation_land_act/
12. www.infoplease.com/ce6/history/A0819828.html
13. Ibid.
14. Melinda Jette, "The Cockstock Incident." *Oregon Historical Quarterly,* 2004. OHQ 4-405-406.
15. McLagan, *Peculiar Paradise,* 50.
16. en.wikipedia.org/wiki/Dred_Scott_v._Sandford
17. Malcolm Clark, Jr., *Eden Seekers: The Settlement of Oregon, 1818–1862* (Boston: Houghton Mifflin, 1981) 290.
18. McLagan, *Peculiar Paradise,* 57.
19. Quintard Taylor, "Slaves and Free Men: Blacks in the Oregon Country, 1840–1860," *Oregon Historical Quarterly* 83:2 (Summer 1982), 169.
20. K. Keith Richard, "Unwelcome Settlers: Black and Mulatto Oregon Pioneers," *Oregon Historical Quarterly* Vol. 83, No.1 (Spring 1983), 37.

21. http://arcweb.sos.state.or.us/echoes/pics/2201.jpg

22. Richard, "Unwelcome Settlers," 51.

23. Martha Hodes, ed., *Sex, Love, Race: Crossing Boundaries in North American History* (New York: New York University Press, 1999).

24. http://en.wikipedia.org/wiki/List_of_Jim_Crow_law_examples_by_State

25. *Oregonian,* 2/8/1868 in Richard, "Unwelcome Settlers," 52.

26. *Oregonian,* 10/7/1868 in Richard, "Unwelcome Settlers," 53.

27. http://www.ode.state.or.us/opportunities/grants/saelp/orracial-laws.pdf

28. "Emancipation Day," *Daily Statesman and Unionist,* 1/4/1870.

29. Susan N. Bell, "Salem's Colored School," *Historic Marion,* Vol. 40, No. 1 (Spring 2002), 8–9.

30. Ibid.

31. en.wikipedia.org/wiki/Plessy_v._Ferguson

Chapter 2

1. Oregon Historical Society Documents vol. III, 1902.

2. www.ohs.org/education/oregonhistory/narratives/subtopic.cfm?subtopic_ID=270

3. Polk County Historical Society informational kiosk, Rickreall.

4. www.webtrail.com/applegate/biography.shtml. "The Applegate Trail—The Men of the South Road Expedition and Their Lives Afterward"

5. www.blackpast.org; Elizabeth McLagan, *A Peculiar Paradise* (Portland: Georgian Press, 1980), 14–17.

6. February 23, 2002, www.suite101.com/article.cfm/caring_soul/89606

7. "A leader along the trail," *Statesman Journal,* 1/22/1994.

8. www.historicoregoncity.org

9. Jerome Peltier, *Black Harris* (Fairfield, WA: Ye Galleon Press, 1986).

10. McLagan, *Peculiar Paradise,* 17.

11. www.oregonpioneers.com

12. Bonter obituary, *Statesman,* 11/11/1915.

13. *Statesman,* 3/4/1870.

14. 1870 Marion County census.

15. *Statesman,* 11/11/1915.

16. Sarah Hunt Steeves, *Book of Remembrance of Marion County, Oregon, Pioneers, 1840–1860* (Portland: Berncliff Press, 1927).

17. en.wikipedia.org/wiki/Mulatto

18. Pioneer Cemetery records; copy of the receipt from "William Delany," administrator of the estate.

19. Marion County census records; she appears in the Delaney household in 1860.

20. *Statesman,* 1/15/1930.

21. *Statesman,* 10/13/1910.

22. Colin Palmer, ed., *The Encyclopedia of African-American Culture and History,* Vol. 4 (Detroit: Macmillan Reference USA, 2006).

23. www.oregonlive.com: 1849: Rose Jackson's trip to Oregon in a box.

24. www.historicoregoncity.org

25. www.oregonpioneers.com

26. Shirley O'Neil, *Polk County Pioneers.* 2002—Oregon State Library 929-379538.

27. http://start-wa.com/wagon_train.html

28. Terri A. Siner, ed., *Rickreall: Coming to the Vale of the Rickreall* (Rickreall, OR, 2000).

29. Pauline Burch manuscripts at the Oregon State Library.

30. O'Neil, *Polk County Pioneers.*

31. www.oregonpioneers.com

32. Burch MSS.

33. Ibid.

34. O'Neil, *Polk County Pioneers.*

35. Burch MSS.

36. Oregon Pioneer Association. Transactions of the fourth annual reunion. Oregon State Library.

37. May Dasch, *Hannah Gorman and Eliza J. Gorman: Early Afro-American Pioneers in Benton County, Oregon.* Paper, February 24, 2004.

38. Crystal Lake Cemetery kiosk.

39. Correspondence with Brian Waldo Johnson, 11/2010.

40. www.salemhistory.net/people/african_americans.htm

41. McLagan, *Peculiar Paradise,* 85.

42. O'Neil, *Polk County Pioneers.*

43. *The Walkers of Spring Valley.* Polk County, OR (n.d.)

44. Stone, Buena (as told to her by Wayne Henry, grandson of Walter Walker), *A Valley of Many Springs: A Story of Walter M. Walker* (Polk County, OR, 2000).

Chapter 3

1. Fred Lockley, ed., "'Documentary': The Case of Robin Holmes vs. Nathaniel Ford." *Oregon Historical Quarterly*, Vol. 23, No. 2 (June 1922), 111–37.
2. "The Cloud of Slavery," *Sunday Oregonian Magazine*, 3/2/1952, 16–17.
3. Pauline Burch MS, "Pioneer Nathaniel Ford and the Negro Family," Oregon State Library.
4. "The Cloud of Slavery"; Mark and Scott drowning: Burch MS.
5. Lockley, "'Documentary,'" 114.
6. en.wikipedia.org/wiki/Ellendale,_Oregon.
7. Burch MS.
8. Lockley, "'Documentary.'"
9. Ibid., 114.
10. Ibid., 118.
11. Scott McArthur, "The Polk County Slave Case." *Historically Speaking, Journal of the Polk County, Oregon, Historical Society*, Vol. 2, August 1970, 5.
12. Lockley, "'Documentary.'"
13. Ibid.
14. "Black Pioneers Settle Oregon Coast," http://ftp. wi.net/~maracon/lesson5.html.
15. Lockley, "'Documentary.'"
16. K. Keith Richard, "Unwelcome Settlers," 29–55.
17. George H. Williams, "Political History of Oregon from 1853 to 1865." *Oregon Historical Quarterly*, Vol. 2, No. 1, 1901, 5–6.
18. "The Cloud of Slavery."
19 K. Keith Richard, "Oregon denied first blacks rights, freedoms." *Eugene Register-Guard*, February 27, 2000, F4.
20. "Cloud of Slavery."
21 Ibid.
22. Burch MS.
23. Ibid.

Chapter 4

1. Steeves, *Book of Remembrance*.
2. Jerry Miller, "Beale and Baker," Macleay Community Club, March 12, 1965.
3. Steeves, *Book of Remembrance*.
4. Trial transcripts in www.oregonpioneers.com/gbtrial.htm.

5. *Peculiar Paradise,* 85.
6. *Statesman Journal,* December 3, 2002.

Chapter 5

1. Egbert S. Oliver, "Obed Dickinson and the 'Negro Question' in Salem," *Oregon Historical Quarterly,* Vol. 92, No. 1 (Spring 1991), 4.
2. Myron Eells, *History of the Congregational Association, 1848–1880* (Portland: Pub. House of Himes the Printer, 1881), 34.
3. Ibid., 35.
4. Oliver, "Obed Dickinson," 10.
5. www.salemhistory.net/people/african_americans.htm
6. *Oregon Statesman,* September 16, 1861.
7. Egbert Oliver, *Obed Dickinson's War Against Sin in Salem* (Portland: Hapi Press, 1987), 139.
8. Ibid.,140.
9. Ibid., 141.
10. Oliver, "Obed Dickinson," 13–14.
11. Ibid., 15.
12. Florence Wells, ed., "The Letters of Asahel Bush to Matthew Deady, 1851–1863." MA theses, Reed College 1941, 165–66, in Richard, "Unwelcome Settlers," 55.
13. Oliver, *Obed Dickinson's War,* 153–54.
14. Ibid., 164–65.
15. Ibid., 166–72.
16. "1820s coverlet and its stories to be preserved at museum," *Statesman Journal,* 8/4/2010.

Chapter 6

1. *Statesman,* 4/19/1907.
2. George S. Trumbull, *History of Oregon Newspapers* (Portland: Binfords & Mort, 1939) 107.
3. www.findagrave.com
4. Sons of Union Veterans of the Civil War: www.suvoregon.org
5. "Enumeration of Inhabitants and Industrial Products" is thought to be part of census records, Oregon State Library.
6. www.family-passages.com/Publications/SouthworthLewis.pdf
7. www.aaregistry.org/historic_events/view/louis-southworth-oregon-pioneer
8. *Congressional Record—Senate,* February 28, 2005: remarks by Sen. Gordon Smith.

9. www.aaregistry.org/historic_events/view/louis-southworth-oregon-pioneer

Chapter 8

1. *Oregonian,* 5/20/05, in Jun Xing et al, eds., *Seeing Color: Indigenous Peoples and Racialized Ethnic Minorities in Oregon* (Lanham, MD: University Press of America, 2007), 79.
2. en.wikipedia.org/wiki/McCants_Stewart#cite_note-OHS-3
3. Jun, *Seeing Color,* 80.
4. Ibid., 84.
5. Ibid., 82–83.
6. *Advocate* 7/12/1930 in Jun, *Seeing Color,* 83.
7. www.salemlf.org. Thanks to Sam Skillern.
8. en.wikipedia.org/wiki/Ben_W._Olcott
9. Milton Meltzer, *The Truth About the Ku Klux Klan* (New York: Franklin Watts, 1982).
10. Jun, *Seeing Color,* 87.
11. Ibid., 88–89.
12. Ibid., 84.
13. Ibid., 85.
14. Ibid., 86.
15. Howard Goodman, "Bigotry: Oregon's Sad History." *Statesman Journal,* 2/8/1981.
16. "Kathryn Hall Bogle's 'An American Negro Speaks of Color'" and Interview: "Kathryn Hall Bogle on the Writing of 'An American Negro Speaks of Color.'" *Oregon Historical Quarterly,* Vol. 89, No. 1 (Spring 1988), 80.
17. Loewen, James W., *Sundown Towns: A Hidden Dimension of American Racism* (New York: New Press, 2005).
18. Goodman, "Bigotry: Oregon's Sad History."
19. *Peculiar Paradise,* 149.
20. www.africawithin.com/bios/paul_robeson.htm
21. Hatfield, Mark O., *Against the Grain: Confessions of a Rebel Republican* (Ashland, OR: White Cloud Press, 2001), 58.
22. Letter from David A. Rhoten, 5/21/2010.
23. Hatfield, *Against the Grain,* 58.
24. Robert E. Colbert, "Current Trends and Events, Section C: The Attitude of Older Negro Residents Toward Recent Negro Migrants in the Pacific Northwest." *The Journal of Negro Education,* Vol. 15, 1946.

25. Kilbourn, Charlotte, and Margaret Lantis, "Elements of Tenant Instability in a War Housing Project," *American Sociological Review,* Vol. 11 (February 1946), 57–66.

26. "Vanport (1942-1948)," www.blackpast.org/?q=aaw/african-american-history-american-west

27. "Vanport Deemed Ghetto," *Oregon Journal,* 3/10/1952.

28. en.wikipedia.org/wiki/Portland,_Oregon

29. U.S. Census.

30. www.portland.com/portland/articles/population-of-portland/

31. www.washington.edu/uwired/outreach/cspn/Website/Class-room%20Materials/Pacific%20Northwest%20History/Lessons/Lesson%2021/21.html

32. www.oregonlink.com/population_history.html

33. Jun, *Seeing Color,* 90.

34. en.wikipedia.org/wiki/Brown_v._Board_of_Education

Chapter 11

1. www.ohs.org/education/oregonhistory/historical_records/dsp-Document.cfm?doc_ID=C699DEE7-A96D-A179-FC22756A21DF898B

2. en.wikipedia.org/wiki/Civil_Rights_Act_of_1964

3. en.wikipedia.org/wiki/Voting_Rights_Act

4. en.wikipedia.org/wiki/Harper_v._Virginia_Board_of_Elections

5. Interview with Pastor Gussie Brown.

6. Interview with Arthur Shankle.

7. http://greencoatplace.org/node/23228

8. 2002 General Election Voters' Pamphlet.

9. http://ballotpedia.org/wiki/index.php/Oregon_Ballot_Measure_14_(2002)

Index

Printed in the USA
CPSIA information can be obtained
at www.ICGtesting.com
LVHW051340010823
754046LV00002B/125